16

THE ANGLER'S GUIDE TO

SEA FISHING

THE ANGLER'S GUIDE TO

SEA FISHING

BILL HOWES

A SALAMANDER BOOK

Published by Salamander Books Ltd
8 Blenheim Court
Brewery Road
London N7 9NT
United Kingdom

© Salamander Books Ltd 1985,1999

ISBN 1 84065 107 5

Front and back cover photographs courtesy of Angling Times
Back cover illustration courtesy of Salamander Picture Library

AUTHOR

Bill Howes began his angling career as a boy, fishing in the local canal.
He progressed to become a skilled all-round angler, and has caught
many fine specimens of coarse, game and sea fish. He has taken part in
many freshwater and sea fishing competitions, and has been a member
– and twice team captain – of seven England teams competing in
international sea angling events. As an angling journalist and
photographer, Bill has written and illustrated hundreds of articles for
the angling press, and has been the author of 15 books on fishing. A
former evening-class instructor on angling techniques,
he has also broadcast on radio and television.

CONSULTANT

Len Cacutt has spent 20 years closely associated with angling
journalism and literature as editor of a number of publications. He was
founder-editor of *Angler's Mail* and editor of *Fisherman's Handbook* and
Fisherman's Weekly, and has acted as editor and consultant
for many angling books.

ACKNOWLEDGMENTS
The author and publishers would like to thank the following for their
contributions to this book: Geoff Bucknall, Paul Cartwright, Ron
Edwards, Ken Fox, John Holden, Trevor Housby, Mike Millman,
Eric Pace, Russ Symons, Peter Wheat, Alan Yates.

CREDITS
Editor: John Woodward
Designer: Tony Dominy
Colour reproductions: Melbourne Graphics
Filmset: SX Composing Ltd.
Printed and bound in Spain by Just Colour Graphic, S. L.

CONTENTS

INTRODUCTION

Each year sees more and more anglers turning to the sea for their sport, attracted by the thrill of adventure which the sea always provides, and the challenge of angling for really big fish. Catches can be very large, and whereas freshwater fishing is often a waiting game demanding considerable skill and patience, obvious to any spectator, it can sometimes look as though the sea angler only has to cast out a bait to be sure of reeling in a fish.

In fact, to stand a good chance of catching fish consistently it is important to use the right bait, tackle and technique. Ideally the angler should always use tackle to suit the type of fishing and the average size of the species. This is not just to ensure a catch – if the sport is to be rewarding it is essential that skill is required.

Generally the line-class ratings of equipment serve as a useful guide to what to use. If 20lb (9kg) fish are expected, use 20lb breaking strain (b.s.) tackle. Such equipment will ensure that the angler gets maximum pleasure from the fight. Unfortunately it is not always possible to use gear which is precisely matched to the fish, because strong tidal currents often demand that heavy weights are used to hold the bait down – and the heavier the weight, the stronger the rest of the tackle has to be.

Most beginners have no idea which fish, even which type of fishing they may eventually want to concentrate on, so the first outfit is inevitably something of a compromise. It is best to start with a general-purpose rod, suitable for both shore and boat fishing – the tackle dealer will advise on this, as on other items of equipment. In time the need will

be felt for at least two rods. The boat angler will need a light outfit and a heavy outfit, and beach anglers need two rods to cope with the demands of different casting distances and casting weights.

Although there are very few restrictions on sea angling, and the individual can fish more or less where he likes, it pays to join a club. Apart from the benefits of companionship and practical advice, this will also allow access to major angling competitions, and makes it easier to join regular charter boat trips.

Small boats are restricted in practise to inshore waters, yet this is a popular section of the sport, with more and more anglers trailing their own craft to the coast. Before taking a small boat to sea, however, it is essential to study the Seaway Code, be aware of hazards in the area, and ensure that the boat has a properly rigged radar reflector. A small boat can be almost invisible from the bridge of a large ship. It is best not to venture too far out, in case the weather worsens, and at all times the boat angler must remain aware of local tide conditions.

The safety of the shore angler can also depend upon the tide. The danger of being cut off when rock or beach fishing is very real, and in rough weather the consequences could be fatal. The safety of others must also be borne in mind. When beach casting make sure the line and knots are sound, because if a lead weight 'cracks off' during the cast it may well kill someone. There are often regulations posted on piers and jetties which prohibit techniques such as overhead casting. Sea fishing does not have to be dangerous to be enjoyable.

TACKLE

RODS

For many years the design of rods for sea fishing remained unchanged, anglers being content to use the rods their forebears used. Most were thick 'billiard cues' of wood and cane.

With the increased efficiency of commercial fishing, which swept up fish in such numbers that anglers found catches hard to come by, more sophisticated tackle and techniques were needed, and we are now experiencing a period of rapid tackle development.

An instance of this is the beachcasting rod. Some years ago the layback method of casting was popular, using a relatively slow-actioned rod with a reverse-taper butt. Then, 100 yards (90m) was an exceptional cast; today anglers look for casts of at least 140 yards (128m) with baited hook, the rods being built with much faster actions to suit the new pendulum, or South African, casting styles.

The new rod material is called semi-carbon: the butt and centre sections are of carbon, and a glass tip is laminated into the carbon top section. Normally, these rods have shortish butt sections of rigid material – alloy, glass or carbon – with the longer top section of about 8ft (2.4m) fitting into the short, stiff butt end. Such rods have swept the board at casting tournaments, using only a weight on the end of a line, gaining distances of over 200 yards (180m).

Boat rods

Boat fishing catches have been much improved by the use of rods designed for casting well away from the boat. In shallow water the vibrations from light, modern fibreglass-hulled craft can scare fish away, so the further the bait is cast from the boat, the better.

These rods are about 9ft (2.7m) long, like the modern beachcasting rod, 9ft being the best length to combine casting facility with the power to pump up a large fish.

There are cheaper models in glass, but modern versions follow the 'semi-carbon' structure of beach rods, with stiff butts for positioning against the side of the boat.

The standard boat rod has undergone little change, the short butt and longer top section conforming to the International Game Fishing Association (IFGA) line classes; from lines of about 12-20lb (5.4-9kg) b.s. for inshore fishing to 30-80lb (13.6-36kg) b.s. for deepwater or wreck fishing. There has been a move towards stiffer actions for setting hooks in deep water, and roller rings to reduce friction from line; these are vital when wire is used.

For the future, it would be a boon to have rods with interchangeable tops of various line ratings for a single butt end. It would also make sense to have the butt end offset, as it is in some bait-casting and spinning rods, so that the spool of the reel is in line with the rod rings to eliminate friction.

REELS

Most boat fishing is done with the multiplier, a complex descendant of the old winch reel. Such reels have geared mechanisms which produce three or four turns of the spool for every turn of the handle. For deepwater sea fishing, specialised reel-makers offer fast-retrieve versions of their large-capacity models, such as the Penn Senator 4/0.

A new family of boat-fishing reels is on the drawing-board, offering the

Above: *This angler is using a medium-sized multiplier reel mounted on a strong boat rod – an outfit suitable for fairly heavy fish.*

facility of quick-change spools and a line distributor which 'floats' freely during line release to reduce friction. The same innovations in design are being applied to the smaller beach-casting reels.

Reels for beachcasters need to be fairly light-spooled multipliers to do their best work. The dedicated caster will often remove the line distributor completely in the quest for greater casting distance, and may strengthen the cage with a specially-made stiffening support bar.

One difficulty when casting with the multiplier is the prevention of overrun. When the tackle hits the water it stops dead, but the spool continues to spin, spilling line into a great tangle – a 'bird's nest'. One way of preventing this is by using the thumb as a brake on the spool. This takes practise, but the problem of overrun can now be overcome by using a reel with a magnetic field to control the speed of the spool.

Until recently the spool of a multiplier could not be removed unless the side-plate screws were undone, leading to the near-dismantling of the reel. The new designs of multiplier allow the spool to be removed and another fitted.

Below: *Most sea fishing rods have the usual bridge or strutted rings (left) but roller tip-rings are often fitted to line-class rods, or rods for use with wire (right). Big-game rods have rollers fitted throughout.*

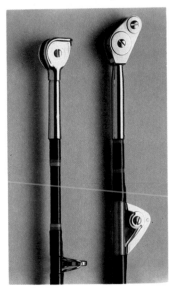

Fixed-spool reel

For those anglers who find the split-second thumb timing needed to prevent multiplier overrun too difficult, the fixed-spool reel has advantages, although such reels are considered to give less casting distance due to the friction as the line coils fly from the drum.

Modern designs have reduced this problem, and the distances gained with large capacity fixed-spool reels do not fall far short of those obtained with the multipliers. The elimination of overrun has made the fixed-spool a favourite for night fishing, when the angler with a multiplier is unable to see when the tackle hits the water, and so when to use his thumb.

Extra distance can be gained by using conical spools, and some models have either no pick-up to fly back accidentally, or else the pick-up can be fixed in the open position.

LINES

There are three types of line used in sea angling: monofilament nylon, braided line and metal or wire line. Most anglers use monofilament for all their fishing, whether from shore or boat. This comes in breaking strains (b.s.) from about 6lb (2.7kg) for mullet and flatfish, to 50 or even 80lb (22.6-36kg) b.s. for sharks.

Nylon line is very thin considering its strength, which makes it ideal for long casting from a beach. Any increase in diameter adds to the line's resistance through the air.

It also has considerable elasticity, which adds to its shock-absorbing capacity when playing a powerful fish. This elasticity can however be a drawback when fishing in deep water. A hundred or more feet (30m) of nylon will stretch and take all the power from a strike. For deep water fishing it is therefore best to use braided line. Its lack of stretch allows direct pressure to be applied to a big fish.

Braided line is soft and pliable and has the advantage that it knots easily and firmly, unlike nylon which slips unless the special knots devised for its use are employed.

A drawback of braided line is its large diameter. This makes it catch the tide more than nylon, so heavier weights are needed to take the tackle down. Even then a strong tide will put a large bow from angler to weight, making a strike difficult.

Wire line

Flexible wire line is noted for its tide-cutting properties, and since it goes straight down to the terminal tackle

Below: *Strong wire traces with heavy-duty swivels are essential for shark fishing. This outfit includes a Penn 6/0 reel, butt pad, and float.*

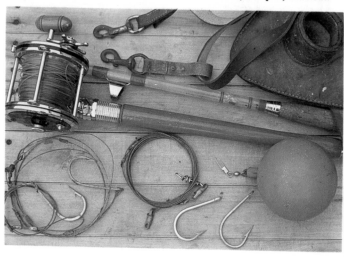

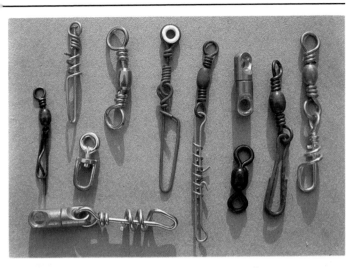

without bowing, the angler can make a positive strike when a fish is felt.

The drawback to wire is that it is not recommended when fishing from a crowded boat. In fact, serious sea anglers never do this unless some circumstance forces them to. The reason is that tangles in wire are ruinous. It needs just one kink to spoil the whole length from there down. Furthermore, wire has to be used with rods fitted with roller rings – it cuts through any other. It can also cut through flesh, including yours. Never take hold of wire when a fish is coming aboard, and never try to free wire by hand when it is fouled on the bottom. Take great care when using it.

TRACES

For most fish, terminal rig traces are made of nylon, often of the same b.s. as the reel line. The main advantage of using a trace in such circumstances is the ease with which rigs can be changed. For some conditions a trace of different b.s. is used, and it may even be made of different material.

The shock-leader

The beachcaster attaches a trace of higher b.s. than the reel line to absorb the shock of casting the lead weight. Known as the shock-leader, it has to be twice the length of the rod, plus a few turns of the reel spool, to be sure of preventing breakage during the

initial, powerful casting swing. A 25-35lb (11.3-16kg) b.s. leader is normally used with 15-18lb (7-8kg) b.s. reel line, but a poor caster should use 45-50lb (20.4-22.6kg) b.s.

Wire traces

Traces can be made from flexible wire for certain fish. Shark, for instance, need traces from 15-20ft (4.5-6m) long from 750lb (340kg) b.s. to as much as 1,000lb (450kg), for their teeth will cut through anything lighter. Yacht-rigging wire is preferred by regular shark anglers.

Conger, tope and spurdog all need wire traces, and the b.s. has to be chosen to suit the species. Each hook trace is made up with a loop for attaching to a quick-release swivel, which itself is joined to an reel line. Metal crimps are used to make strong connections in the wire.

SWIVELS

When spinning it is vital to fit swivels between reel line and lure to prevent severe line twist. Even a non-spinning rig should have at least one swivel in it, and long shark traces will have at least four.

Swivels are also useful for connecting sections of line and trace, and assembling terminal rigs. They are available in a variety of styles and patterns, including simple double-ended types, three-way swivels for attaching snoods, quick-release spring, snap and buckle types, and heavy-duty swivels for really big fish.

Unfortunately, many of the swivels in the tackleshops are not designed to suit fishing conditions round the northern European coasts. Some are too weak, and require careful testing before use; some too small or not sufficiently rustproof.

When selecting swivels from the tacklebox, check for signs of rust. Not only will the strength have been reduced, but the free-turning ability will suffer from friction and the swivel may eventually fracture.

BOOMS
Booms for paternoster and running leger links are essential, the most useful types being Clement's, Kilmore, threeway swivel, flexi-, French and special long wire booms.

Below: *A selection of popular booms, including Kilmore (left) and Clement's booms with hard-wearing ring inserts. The others are variations on the Clement's design.*

Other useful items of terminal tackle are line clips or bait-safes. These enable the beachcaster to deliver an undamaged soft bait to the chosen area at long range. When the terminal tackle reaches the target the bait is freed, to act in the normal way.

FLOATS
The function of a float is to support a bait at the required depth; when a fish takes the offering the float then registers the bite.

Floats are not used very often in sea fishing, but sharking employs them as does fishing for garfish, mullet and wrasse.

Both fixed and slider floats can be used in the sea, the slider being very useful at the depths in which much sea fishing is carried out. The larger floats used in freshwater fishing are quite adequate for most purposes, particularly the slimmer models of pike floats.

WEIGHTS
Lead weights or sinkers come in a variety of shapes known as pyramids, Capta leads, conical and pear-shaped leads, and Arlesey bombs; then there are flat grip-leads, wire grapnel leads such as the breakaway, and anchor leads. All have their special uses, but for general sea fishing on the bottom

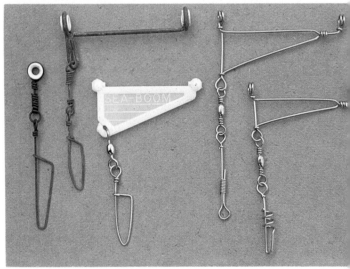

the circular grip lead and the conical leads are used more than the others.

There are also anti-kink leads for use when spinning, which prevent line twist. Popular models are the Wye spinning lead and the Jardine spiral lead.

Grapnel leads are useful in tide runs, the most popular being those with springy steel or brass grip wires attached to the nose. On breakaway types the wires spring back into a trailing position if the line is pulled hard, allowing the lead to be dislodged when necessary. This ensures that the weight cannot foul in rough ground.

Above: *The grip wires of a breakaway lead are held in place by beads lodged in cavities. When a fish pulls on the bait the wires spring back and the weight is free.*

Below: *A selection of lead weights:* ① *Conical lead with two eyes, for use without a boom.* ② *Pear-shaped lead.* ③ *Capta, shaped to sit firmly on the bottom when used in a current.* ④ *Circular grip lead.* ⑤ *Grapnel lead with springy grip wires which dig into the seabed.* ⑥ *A small No. 4 circular grip lead.* ⑦ *Flat-sided torpedo casting lead.*

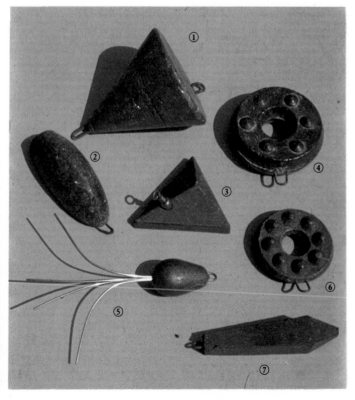

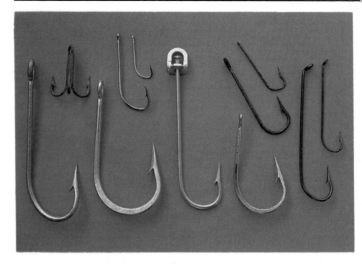

Above: *A range of hooks to suit most sizes of bait and fish, including long- and short-shanked patterns, a swivelled hook for conger fishing (centre), and a small treble hook for use on a lure (top left).*

HOOKS

It is a false economy to buy cheap hooks – they are the main link with the fish and that link must hold.

Hooks can be purchased loose, a few at a time, or in boxes of a 100 or so. They can be obtained already tied or mounted to wire or nylon snoods. Most anglers, however, prefer to tie on their own.

Get your hooks from dealers who sell the reputable brands, and seek advice if you are unsure which sizes, models or styles you want for your particular preference in fishing. They are available in a huge range of sizes. They can be long or short shanked, the barb can be straight or offset, and the eye can be turned up or down. The section may be square or round, and some patterns have nicks on the shank to hold a bait such as lugworm and prevent it slipping down to the bend.

Maintenance

Anglers hook fewer fish than they should because their hooks are not sharp. Straight from the shop, very few hooks are needle-sharp, in fact a high proportion are distinctly blunt.

Make a habit of checking the point of every hook before putting it on the line. Then make another check every half-dozen casts. At the first sign of damage or bluntness touch it up with the small carborundum stone which should be in every tackle box.

BUTT PAD

A groin or stomach protector in the form of a butt pad is a very useful accessory. It fits on a belt and is merely a metal or leather pouch which supports the rod butt when you are fighting a large, powerful fish. It is essential for boat anglers fishing very deep water with heavy tackle, particularly for conger or big skate. Trying to haul one of these very strong fish from the depths can be strain on man and tackle, and the butt pad ensures that no effort is wasted.

A full harness, which not only supports the angler's rod but also ensures that he cannot lose it, is worn by tunny and marlin fishermen in non-European waters, and by the shark angler who likes to play safe.

ROD RESTS

A rod rest is essential for the beach or shore angler. Even the bass fisherman, who likes to hold the rod while feeling for bites, needs a rest to support the rod while he is baiting up or changing some item on the terminal rig.

There are single-leg, monopod and tripod rests; some push into the sand or gravel, some rest on shovel-like supports. They must all be strong enough to support long beachcasting rods, and withstand the pull of the tide when it swirls round the legs.

Above: *Substantial rod rests should be part of every angler's outfit; they are essential with two rods.*

Below: *A tripod rest supports the rod while the angler displays a fine greater spotted dogfish.*

and tail fins and simply heave it over the side to remove the hooks.

For anglers not yet ready to do this, the salmon tailer is another useful item. A stout noose can also be used, but care must be taken not to cause harm to the fish.

GAFFS

When finally brought to the boat, many sea fish are too large to be lifted out by hand, or the hook-hold may be too slim to take chances with it. In such cases a gaff is needed. Some species such as conger must be gaffed, as they are too dangerous to try to manhandle inboard.

The screw-in gaff head used in freshwater is too weak for sea fishing. Here, the gaff head must be firmly lashed or clamped to a stout handle, the length of which depends on the boat it is kept on.

Shark and big-game fishing needs a flying gaff. This implement has a head

Above: *When fishing from a high pier or breakwater a normal landing net will not reach the water. Here the angler is using a drop net to gather up the fish.*

Below: *A charterboat skipper uses a gaff to get a monkfish aboard. The gaff is hooked under the lower jaw of the fish so it can be returned alive to the water.*

For boat anglers and pier fishermen there are special rod rests which can be clamped or strapped to the rails.

LANDING NETS AND DROP NETS

Landing nets for sea fishing must be robust and larger than those used in freshwater. Any fish that is to be returned alive, other than tope, should be brought aboard with a landing net, as should any fish hooked on light line.

A dropnet is a square or circular net designed to be lowered from a position high above the water. A bicycle wheel rim is about the right size; fitted with strong mesh and four cords linked to a long rope, it makes a very useful net.

In these days of conservation-minded anglers, tope are usually returned to the water unharmed, as are small blue sharks. A gaff cannot be used, and the usual landing net is too flimsy. Experts anglers can tail tope – that is grasp the fish by the pectoral

BOXES AND CONTAINERS

Lugworm, ragworm, and mackerel must be kept separate when they are being carried to the boat or beach. Plastic boxes are ideal for most items, and a picnic cold-box will keep the bait cold and fresh for the day.

A haversack is useful for carrying bait boxes, weights, and accessories that will not be affected by the sea spray that gets everywhere on a boat.

Steel boxes do not make suitable containers for tackle because they are subject to rust. Plastic or polythene is the ideal material, and the smaller boxes are excellent for holding swivels, hooks, booms and leger links. These items are best kept separate otherwise they end up as a tangled heap that takes ages to sort out.

Large bottle corks are ideal for hooks, the points lightly inserted to keep them clean.

There are specialist tackle boxes available with cantilevered trays, and since they are made in strong plastic they are ideal for sea fishing. The larger models have six or seven trays with over 50 partitions for small accessories. At the bottom of the box

Above: *A well-designed tackle box enables the angler to change rigs quickly and efficiently, and reduces the chances of delicate items getting damaged in transit.*

which is detachable from the handle, but which remains attached by a length of very strong nylon. An important point is that this rope must be fixed to the boat, and never held.

Below: *Artery forceps (bottom) are invaluable for removing hooks. Stubborn cases may need pliers – the combination plier and crimping tool (top) is useful, as is a knife.*

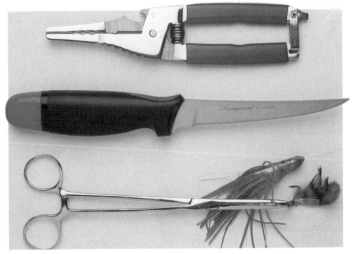

there is space for spare reels, spools of line and other bulky items.

Many sea anglers acquire large seat-boxes which not only hold a lot of gear but provide a seat. But all the boxes and containers described must be watertight and proof against corrosion by seawater.

SUNDRIES

Anglers should always carry a knife. It should be razor-sharp to produce clean, fine fillets and strips of fresh fish. The traditional scout's knife is not suitable, and the best pattern is a proper filleting knife or a small butcher's knife. Be sure to sharpen a good-quality blade before every trip.

Polarized sunglasses are an asset if you happen to be sitting facing the full glare of a summer sun; they eliminate the distracting sparkles that come off the water.

A crimping tool is essential for anglers who use wire traces. Long-nosed pliers and artery forceps will help remove hooks from bony jaws.

CLOTHING

The shore angler and the boat fisherman should always have some warm clothing available, even when starting out on a warm summer's day. Waterproof clothing is essential for the boat angler, for although the weather may be fine at the start of the trip, it can change very suddenly – and there is nowhere to go in an open boat when it is pouring with rain.

The ubiquitous wellington boots are fine for many angling situations, but there are occasions when they should not be worn. One of these is when fishing from weed-covered rocks and other slippery places, and the other is when beachcasting, for it is pretty certain that at some time you will need to wade out – and a wellie full of cold seawater on a winter's night is no joke. Here, thigh-length or chest-high waders are the only solution.

When boat fishing, never wear studded boots, because they can cause expensive damage to wooden decks. In warm weather canvas rubber-soled shoes are fine. In cold weather you will need good waterproof shoes that will also give a firm grip on wet decks.

KNOTS

Every angler must learn to tie a few knots, and in the case of nylon these knots must be of a special type that will not slip. A badly tied knot in nylon not only slips, it considerably reduces the b.s. of the line.

Nylon is an extremely smooth material, which is the reason why it tends to slip when tied wrongly; it also stretches and can cut through itself if the knot is wrongly tied.

The tucked half-blood is handy for tying nylon to any items of tackle that

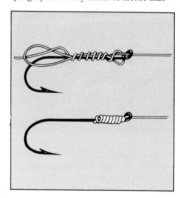

Domhof knot: *For attaching a hook. Thread the line through the eye and lay a loop along the shank. Whip the free end eight times round hook and line, and through the loop.*

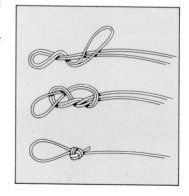

Blood bight: *A simple, strong way of forming a loop. Bend the nylon double, and twist the looped end twice round and back through. Pull tight and trim the loose end.*

have eyed ends, such as hooks, swivels, lures and so on. The free end of nylon protruding from the knot should be clipped off, otherwise it tends to snag on rod rings and other items of terminal tackle.

A simple paternoster can be made by tying-in three loops. Check where they are to go, then slacken off the trace and form a loop by means of the double overhand loop knot – twisting the loop round itself twice, then tucking the end loop back through and pulling tight. A similar loop in the

hook snood can be attached by passing the paternoster loop through the snood loop, then threading the hook end of the snood through the paternoster loop. This produces a two-loop knot which can be pulled tight. It is a useful knot, allowing quick changing of rigs without tying and untying.

Knots are not used in wire traces, all connections being made by metal sleeves called crimps. A special crimping tool is used to make the necessary non-slip connections.

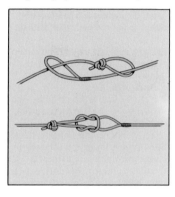

Two loops: *A cheap, effective way to attach a snood. Pass the loop of a blood bight through that of a bloodloop dropper, then pass the hook through the blood bight.*

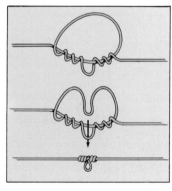

Bloodloop dropper: *Use when rigging a paternoster. Make a loop and twist the free end round the other five or more times. Push the loop through the centre twist.*

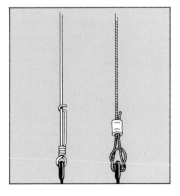

Wire trace fixings: *With flexible wire (left) pass it through the eye twice, thread it through the loop, and crimp. Stiff wire (right), used for bait mounting, needs no crimp.*

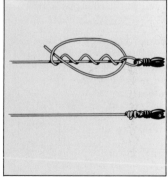

Tucked half blood knot: *For attaching a swivel. Thread the end through the eye, twist it four times round the line, through the loop and back through the knot.*

BAITS

Most saltwater fishes are predatory, feeding on other fishes and often on their own kind as well as practically all the animals that share their environment – gastropods, bivalves, cephalopods, crustaceans, marine worms, starfishes and the tiny and immature forms of them all. They all form part of the diet of fishes.

Obviously, then, they can all be used as bait, some at all times of the year, others only when they are available. Some are effective only in certain circumstances, while others which are known to be eaten by fish never for some reason work when used as hookbait.

Lugworm

Many anglers consider that none of the natural baits is the equal of the lugworm, and this is certainly the best bait for cod, whiting, pouting, flatfish and occasionally other species.

Many anglers prefer to collect their own supply of lug for the day's sport, and in order to find sufficient a good worm-bed must be located. The lug makes a U-shaped burrow in the silt or muddy sand and when the tide recedes it leaves a surface indication in the form of a cast.

A broad-bladed garden spade should be used, dug into the sand at least a foot deep, near the cast. With luck, a lively and undamaged worm will come up as the sand is lifted.

In many places lugworm are becoming scarce, the known beds

Below: *A lugworm bed can be easily recognised by the coiled casts on the surface which the worms eject from their burrows.*

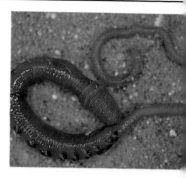

Above: *One of the most popular baits, the lugworm is particularly effective for cod and small flatfish.*

being turned over too often by anglers and professional bait diggers, and because of this it is best to take just enough for the day.

Keep the worms in a shallow wooden container. Do not use metal, for it kills the worms.

Temperature is the important factor deciding how long you will be able to keep lugworm. In winter there is usually no problem, but during a hot spell, lug turn into a foul smelly mass in a few hours.

Worms which are to be kept for a day or two should be laid on newspaper to soak up the excess moisture. Keep them separate by rolling the paper up after each worm has been laid on it, then put it somewhere cool.

When you get on the boat or by the sea, put the day's supply of worms in a container of seawater, for this helps to keep them in good condition.

For the best results, good presentation of any bait is vital – sharking apart – and this means careful hooking. Push the hook into a big worm by threading it up the shank and partly on to the line. Bring the hookpoint out carefully about halfway down, leaving one end to wriggle.

Ragworm

This is a good bait fished from beach, rocks, piers, breakwaters and in harbours and estuaries. There are several species of ragworm, known to anglers as white rag, harbour rag, red and king rag, Largest is the king rag,

Above: *A king ragworm may be used whole for big fish, threaded on to the line with a baiting needle. The hook point is left exposed.*

reaching 12-18in (30-45cm) long, but the standard rag is reddish and measures about 4in (10cm).

Ragworms have two rows of bristles along the sides, and a pair of sharp-pointed pincers on the head which can give a painful nip.

These worms do not leave wormcasts in the mud of harbours, creeks and foreshores, but they can be dug for in much the same way as lug.

Ragworm keep well in any wooden container but plastic will do if the worms are kept moist.

The long king rag can be cut into sections as bait, and used whole when big fish are the quarry. The smaller rag can be used singly or in bunches.

All inshore species can be caught using ragworm, especially bass.

Crab: peelers and softbacks

Crabs are crustaceans, having no internal skeleton, but an outer, crusty shell-like covering. In order to grow larger, crabs have to discard their outer shell and grow a new, larger one, and while the new one hardens the crab is very vulnerable to predators. During this soft period a crab is known as a peeler and then a softie. In these stages it makes a fine bait.

To collect peelers and softbacks, search for their hiding places in rock pools, under rocks, crevices and in thick clumps of weed. To find out if the crab is a peeler, hold it across the back and behind the large claws and try to lift a segment of the shell with a fingernail. A softback is tested simply by prodding the shell on the back. Kept cool, and covered with wet seaweed or a piece of wet sacking, the crabs will live for a day or so.

Crabs can be used whole or in bits, depending on the size of the animal and the hook. When whole, a crab can be threaded onto the hook, and a piece of elasticated thread will keep it safe during a long cast. The legs and claws can be removed and used separately.

If supplies are low, or if a small bait is needed, the body of the crab can be cut in half. Put the body piece on the hook and add some legs, making sure that the point of the hook is exposed. This may not look natural to the angler, but when fished on a long flowing trace it does catch fish.

Hermit crab

This crab makes its home in an empty whelk shell, so where there are whelks there are hermit crabs. As the crab grows, it selects a larger shell. The moment of changeover is critical for when exposed its soft body is very vulnerable to attack.

Hermit crabs can be collected by lowering a baited dropnet off a pier or

Below: *Removed from its shell, a well-presented hermit crab makes a tempting morsel for a big fish.*

jetty, and dinghy anglers usually collect them before moving off to the fishing mark.

This bait must be fished alive and removed from its shell. Fish can be taken on dead ones, but they must still be fresh when the session begins.

Leave them in their shells until ready to bait up, keeping them in a bucket of seawater which should be changed from time to time.

To remove them from the shell, crack it with a light hammer, being careful not to kill the crab. Leave the legs and claws on the crab when fishing for smooth hound, cod, spurdog, large whiting, rays, turbot and bass.

When fishing for black bream and the small flatties, remove the legs and claws and use the soft abdomen and long 'tail' on a long flowing trace.

Squid

It is rare that squid can be caught live for bait, although on occasion a small octopus has been boated while clinging to a baited hook. But squid is very plentiful from fishmongers, and it makes a fine bait.

It can be presented on a hook in a number of ways. Small squid, packed

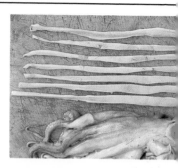

Above: *The body sac of a large squid can be cut into strips. These are very attractive to flatfish.*

in cartons for human consumption, can be used whole to catch rays.

The head and tentacles can be removed to make an attractive hookbait. If they are pulled off rather than being cut off the result is more interesting to feeding fish. The head part can be cut in half to provide two small bunches of tentacles.

The tentacles may be cut off and used singly, especially when match fishing for small whiting, pouting or bream. A single tentacle is an ideal size for these fish to mouth, and it is also tough enough to withstand the attacks of more than one fish while they are being caught and played. Rebaiting is not necessary.

Apart from small squid, the larger squid and cuttlefish can also be used to

Below: *Squid can be presented as a bunch of tentacles* (left), *head and tentacles only* (right), *or whole for big fish such as conger.*

advantage. In conjunction with lugworm they make a good cocktail bait for cod and big whiting.

Thin, tapered strips of squid cut from the body sac are put on the hook first, passing one end up the shank and over the eye. The worm is then threaded onto the hook.

An alternative is to hook the lug first and tip the hook with squid strip, a good idea when beachcasting.

Mussel

Of all the shellfish, mussels are the most prolific, being found in dense clusters all along the coastline, wherever they can get a hold. Their flesh is good for cod, haddock and bream. Mussels can be kept alive for a few days by being put in a container with plenty of damp seaweed.

To use, open the shell and cut the flesh. The hook is inserted in the tough gristly piece at one end.

Above: *A sharp, strong knife is needed to prepare mussels for bait. Slip it between the two shells and lever them apart to reveal the meat (below) which can then be cut out and placed on the hook.*

Whelk

This is a common sea snail with a shell that can reach 6in (15cm) long. Despite its large, strong shell it forms a natural food for bottom-feeding fish such as flatfish.

A drop-net baited with old fish will collect whelks, which are really best when fresh. The net might also bring in a few hermit crabs too. Whelks can be obtained from fishmongers, but they are never as fresh as when caught the same day.

Remove the animal from its shell by cracking the strong shell with a stone or a hammer. Before putting it on the hook remove the round, leathery disc that the whelk uses to protect it when closed up inside.

The body is tough and has good hookholding properties. It stays on the shank when used with a beachcaster, and even stays put in a strong rip-tide. Up to three whelks can be put on one hook, a good tasty mouthful for a roving cod.

Cockle

Another shellfish with two hinged shells, the cockle makes a good change bait when others fail to work. They live partly buried in soft sand or mud and are best collected at low tide. Cockles are never found above highwater mark.

Small holes in the sand indicate where cockles are and they usually congregate in considerable numbers in certain areas. The best tool for collecting them is a small rake.

There is very little in a cockle that stays on a hook, and this makes casting with a fresh cockle almost impossible. A way to deal with this is to collect a supply a day or two before they are needed. Remove the animals from their shells and soak them in a salt and water solution for a few hours. This toughens them so that they stay on the hook better.

Another way is to drop the whole cockles into a pan of really hot water. This kills them instantly, causes the shells to open and at the same time toughens the flesh.

All surplus cockles, minus their shells, can be deep-frozen. Use fine-wire hooks to carry two or three cockles; as a bait they attract bream, flatties, pouting and a variety of other small species.

Razorfish

This long shellfish lives in the sand, and betrays its presence by blowing a jet of water out as it breathes, or when disturbed.

A hooked metal rod is used to extract razorfish from the sand. The hook part enters the shell as it probes, and as it does so the shells close over it. This allows the creature to be pulled to the surface.

When extracted from the paired shells the body makes a good bait for bass, the tough, fleshy foot staying well on the hook.

Above: *The razorfish, or razorshell, has a very large muscular foot which forms a good mouthful for a bass, and stays on the hook well.*

Limpets and slipper limpets

These two shellfish can be easily distinguished by the shell. Common limpets have conical shells which can be seen in thousands on rocks at low tide. The slipper limpet has a shell shaped like a slipper.

A strong-bladed knife is necessary to prise common limpets off the rocks, and they keep up to a fortnight if spread out and stored in a cool place.

The slipper limpet makes the better bait, singly or in bunches, for plaice, dabs, flounders and occasionally bass.

Above: *Cooked shrimps and prawns are easy to obtain and make a useful if comparatively expensive bait for a variety of species.*

Prawns and shrimps

These crustaceans can be gathered inshore, using small-meshed nets which are worked by being pushed slowly along parallel to the shore.

Wear waders when netting these creatures because they occupy the same inshore areas as the lesser weever. This is a venomous fish which can inflict a very painful wound in a bare foot.

Traps lowered from piers will also catch a few prawns, attracted to food items on the mesh.

A container of seawater and fresh seaweed will keep prawns and shrimps alive during the day's fishing if left in a shady place. If the container has a lid with small holes, it can be kept in a keepnet in the sea – the best place for any livebait.

Hook the bait by passing the point of a fine-wire hook through the tail segments from underneath, with the point exposed. This allows the bait to move freely and if the point comes out on the top it seems to aid positive hooking of fish.

Cooked prawns from seafood shops make fine baits for bass, bream and flatties, providing they are not all eaten by the angler or his friends before he starts fishing in earnest.

Mackerel and herring

While the flesh of most fish species can be used as bait, the oily flesh of the mackerel and herring makes them particularly effective. They are used in fillets, halves (heads and tails) or as whole fish when deepsea angling and shark fishing.

Herring are not often caught by angling methods, but they are available from fishmongers. Traces of feathered hooks are ideal for collecting sufficient mackerel for the day's fishing, and there will often be enough for the angler to take some home for dinner afterwards!

A sharp knife must be used to cut mackerel fillets into small, thin slices. Cut them according to the size of the

fish sought and the species. A tiny sliver will do for pouting, using a small hook, while a large hook with a whole mackerel is the bait for shark. The head alone, after the fillets have been removed, is often all that is needed for tope, conger and thornback ray.

Whole sides of mackerel are used for tope, conger and large dogfish, the bait being cut from behind the pectoral fin down to the tail. For most of the smaller species that same fillet can be cut diagonally into thin slices.

Sandeel

There are two species of sandeel, the lesser and the greater, or launce. Both live in the sand, burrowing quickly using their shovel-like jaws.

These small fish are prolific in certain areas, living in huge shoals in

Left: *Herring from the fishmonger are very efficient as bait, whether used whole for big fish such as shark, or in halves or fillets.*

Below: *Cut into slices or fillets, a mackerel still proves almost irresistable to predatory fish.*

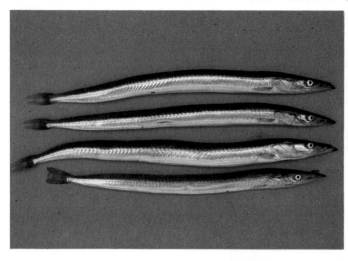

Above: *Sandeels form a major part of the diet of many fish, so they are a natural choice for use as bait.*

sandy bays and estuaries. Coastal sandy beaches generally hold the lesser species, and some anglers consider them the better of the two for use as baitfish.   The angler can collect enough sandeels for a day's fishing by taking an ordinary garden rake to the shore and fitting some fine mesh behind the rake head. Alternatively there is the traditional metal sickle-shaped hook which is

Below: *Normally fished as livebait, sandeels can also be cut into two long fillets. This bait is often very attractive to large flatfish.*

worked through the sand in the shallow water. Short sharp strokes make the sandeels leap clear and they must be collected very fast, for they can disappear into the sand as fast as they left it! Two anglers working together can reduce the problem. One does the raking while the other grabs the eels as they leap out.

A bucket of seawater can be used to hold the sandeels, but they will not survive long and a dead sandeel does not make a decent bait. Dedicated sandeel anglers keep them in specially made boxes which float partly submerged in the sea. Small holes allow fresh seawater to flow through and keep the small fish alive, fresh and attractive to the quarry.

A sandeel can be hooked in its tough protruding lower jaw; another method is to pass the hook through the lip and then lightly through the dorsal area. An alternative is a two-hook trace. A small hook is tied to the line above a larger hook; this enables the sandeel to be lip-hooked, while the reel-line hook is put through the dorsal area. When using the larger species two long fillets can be cut from the body, to act as bait for almost any species of sporting fish.

It is not easy to fish a live sandeel when beachcasting. The moment of striking the water usually kills the bait, but at least you know that it is absolutely fresh.

Above: *Smelt are just one of the many smaller species that make excellent baitfish on occasion.*

Sprat

This small fish is always worth trying as a bait, for sometimes it works well. In season they can be obtained in quantity from fishmongers or baitdealers.

One or even two whole sprats can be mounted on a hook for winter cod. These large-mouthed fish are very partial to sprats and attack shoals of the silvery fish when feeding – which is most of the time.

Sprats yield small, thin fillets, but a very sharp knife is needed. Both fillets can be put on the same hook.

This bait is ideal for dinghy fishing, when the sprat is hooked through both eyes. As a change the hook can be passed through the tail. A baiting needle can be used to thread the hook trace through the fish from tail to head; then a long-shanked hook is attached and drawn back into the mouth, leaving the barb protruding.

If you are beachfishing, a length of cotton or elasticated thread will secure the sprat to the hook.

Sardines

These can be used in the same way as sprats. Any small fish can be put to use as a bait in various ways, and the fresher they are the better. All prove effective at times; fish when feeding are more concerned with engulfing food than deciding what it is.

Artificial lures

The most popular of the artificial lures used in sea angling are the plastic or rubber sandeels of the Redgill type. They come in all sizes and colours – green, blue, yellow, brown and black. For some reason different areas seem to favour certain colours, so it is wise to carry a selection in the tackle box. These lures can be trolled, cast with a spinning outfit or jigged.

Other imitation fish lures are the Rascals and Reefers, which are useful patterns for wreck fishing. The artificial squid, coloured or luminous, are used on their own or in combination with natural baits.

The simple flounder spoon is an old and very successful lure and can be fished under a float, trolled or legered in a strong tide. Another lure with a well-established reputation is the mackerel spinner, which is still made in its traditional shape.

The German Sprat is a particularly popular lure. It is fished in a jerky sink-and-draw style to make its chromium-plated body flash like a sandeel. This lure is really a small kind of pirk, a heavy metal lure made in weights of up to 2lb (0.9kg). Pirks are normally worked among wrecks for pollack and coalfish.

Most of the lures used in freshwater fishing can be employed at sea for bass, mullet and inshore species. A narrow 4in (100cm) silver spinner is an ideal lure for bass when they are chasing sprats.

There are many different types of plug for sea fishing, and the best are those that dive. A built-in vane pushes the nose down as the plug is retrieved whereas if the angler stops winding the plug floats to the surface.

GROUNDBAIT

The reason for groundbaiting is to attract fish to the hookbait. This is true both in fresh and saltwater, and more sea groundbaiting is done than i generally realised.

However, unlike freshwater groundbait, for which the ingredients

Below: *Feathers are a traditional lure for mackerel, but they can also be used to great effect for bream, cod and pollack. A three-hook rig is normally used for the larger species, but for mackerel six feathered hooks are paternostered from a weighted trace, and jigged up and down through the shoal.*

Right: *A selection of artificial lures, designed to imitate mackerel, sandeel, octopus, small fish and squid. They can be used on their own or in combination with natural hookbaits such as lug or squid.*

and recipes are numerous, in the sea the basic material is always the same, with a few odd items added to suit personal or local requirements, the means of introducing the bait, or the known preferences of the quarry.

A groundbait mixture will usually be made up from any fish pieces, such as guts, heads, and leftovers from the bait board – even unwanted sandwiches!

For general fishing a net-bag of fish pieces may be tied to the anchor. The small bits are broken up and washed out by the tide, to trickle along the seabed and attract rays, dogfish, tope and other bottom feeders.

The net-bag can also be used effectively from a pier or breakwater. Here, though, the crab population will soon scurry round to enjoy the unexpected feast.

When fishing from a small boat over a fairly shallow mark, groundbait can be introduced in paper bags. The standard mixture can be employed, plus a few stones to get the bags down quickly. In the water the paper soon splits and the groundbait is released.

Where to drop the bags depends on the strength of tide and the depth. Watch the first bag drop in and judge its route; then the positioning of the next bag can be amended to allow for errors in the first throw. Sometimes the position of the bag on the seabed can be located by oily droplets popping up on the surface.

Mullet often come right in close to harbour walls, pier supports and so on, and because of this the specialist angler devises his own 'secret' mixture, which will contain a variety of ingredients. The most important factor, whatever unusual recipe is used, is that the end product must have a highly pungent odour and contain plenty of tempting morsels.

A favourite recipe includes ancient, minced herrings and/or mackerel, soaked bread and a liberal swig of pilchard oil, plus hookbait samples. This repellent thick liquid groundbait can be put into the sea with a ladle, or a tin can be fitted with a handle.

If preferred, a thicker mixture can be produced, which can be sent to the bottom in a net-bag weighted with a few big stones.

Rubby-dubby

Shark anglers use an attractor in the form of rubby-dubby, which is just a shark angler's term for groundbait. It is the mixture as before, with a bias towards oily fish. These are put through a mincer, and everything mixed, pounded and mashed in a large container. Additional material such as bran and pilchard oil, and blood from a slaughter-house if it can be obtained, will add to the rubby-dubby's shark-attracting powers. The mixture is normally introduced into the water by filling a net-bag which is hung over the side of the boat.

WATERS

SURF BEACHES

A surf beach in rough, windy weather, with white foaming rollers thundering in, is always an exhilarating place, and it is at such times that the beach fishing is usually at its best. The breakers scour and wash many creatures out of the sand, bringing hungry fish right in with the surf. Lesser sandeels and small fish fry congregate just beyond the breakers, attracting bass, plaice and flounder.

The slope of the beach determines the casting distance. Long casting is needed on gently-shelving beaches, and medium-distance casting on the steeper banks. Regular surf beach anglers say that the best area to cast to is just behind the third breaker where the water is usually about 3ft (90cm) deep. This is where the bass will be feeding.

The keen long-distance caster often places his bait too far out, well past the bass, and the angler who cannot cast as far usually catches more fish! But the casting expert gets a bonus when he hooks a ray that can sometimes venture into the area.

A good time to fish a surfbeach is a couple of days after an onshore gale has stirred up the bottom. Offshore winds tend to flatten the surf, and the only fish likely to be caught are the smaller flatties.

The prime time for an exciting session of surf-fishing is at night, but a word of warning is necessary. Keep a watchful eye out for holes when

wading into the surf. Waders full of water make struggling out of strong surf very difficult, and at night there may be no-one nearby to help.

ROCK FISHING

The water off rocky promontories is favoured by many of the popular angling species, including wrasse, bass, mullet, mackerel, pollack and coalfish. They feed down among the

Below: The breaking waves on a surf beach stir up the sand, disturbing small animals which attract fish.

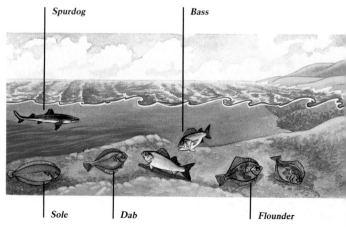

Spurdog   *Bass*

Sole   *Dab*   *Flounder*

Left: Beach fishing demands casting skill, particularly in calm waters when the fish are further out.

rocks, just off the weed surface, and float tackle is often the best way of presenting the bait. The usual leger rig will quickly become snagged in weed or a crevice.

When there is a strong tide flow, it is important to choose a weight which will get the bait down quickly. The float is then chosen to support the end tackle at the right depth. There is often quite deep water off rocks, and a slider float is best in these circumstances.

Some rocky areas hold excellent conger, but catching these involves the risky business of fishing a bait on the bottom. It is best to use a running leger with the weight attached by a nylon link of lower b.s. – a rotten-bottom. If there is not much tide a combination of float and leger can be used, adjusted so that the weight and bait are fished just off the bottom. There will be less risk of a snag, and the fish will find the bait by scent.

Right: Fishing from a rocky promontory can be rewarding, but it can also be dangerous. Proper footwear must be worn.

Below: Wrasse and mullet are attracted to rocky pools. In these sheltered conditions float fishing or spinning can be good techniques.

Rocks are dangerous places. They are often slippery, and proper footwear with effective gripping soles is essential. Take care when clambering over rocks, and always be aware of the state of the tide, and the possibility of being cut off. It is always best to fish with other anglers, or in a place which is well-frequented. A minor accident can quickly become a tragedy if help is not available.

Bass   Mullet   Flounder

ESTUARIES

An estuary is the mouth of a tidal river, and because of the effects of the tide, some skill is needed to judge the right time to fish. There is no hard and fast rule – every estuary is different. Usually, a rising tide is right for fishing over mudflats, particularly for flounders as they move about feeding on worms. The baited spoon rig was devised with this in mind.

Mussels and other shellfish, shrimps and small crabs live in estuaries, attracting a wide variety of fish. Broad expanses of sand covered by the tide often hold sandeels which attract bass and rays.

A few estuaries hold really large fish: 50lb (22.6kg) monkfish, 40lb (18kg) tope, and 20lb (9kg) cod. Some are noted for big skate, but overfishing at the more popular marks has reduced the numbers of such fish caught in these waters.

PIERS AND BREAKWATERS

Some anglers who enjoy fishing for deepwater species find that their pleasure is ruined by the harrowing effects of sea sickness. For these unfortunates, piers, jetties and breakwaters offer a stable platform, and if the site is chosen carefully the angler will be able to fish in deepwater without long casting.

Every coastline has some kind of projection from which an angler can fish, and the only planning necessary is to check the state of tide during the fishing period. Much depends upon

Above: *Estuaries usually harbour vast numbers of shellfish and worms, which are fed on by many fish. Some venture well upriver.*

the tide, not only its depth and speed, but its duration. The time of arrival at the venue should be timed to allow fishing the incoming tide. An ill-judged arrival may see almost dry land at the end of the pier, or nothing but seaweed-covered rocks where there should be waves.

When this happens, make the best of it. You can take advantage of the situation by getting to know the nature of the seabed where you intend to fish when it is covered. Note any patches of sand, rocky areas, thick beds of weed, depressions, and possible tackle traps in the form of sunken boats, rusting rubbish and so on.

There are always fish in the vicinity of these coastal structures. They lurk in the security of the pilings and supports of piers, or crevices in breakwaters and rocks. Where bass and mullet are concerned, there is more chance of catching them in these areas than from an expensive charterboat several miles offshore.

The concrete piers and breakwaters often hold a few conger, which can grow very large lurking in holes in the bases of these structures. You only have to drop a large bait straight down – and hope it is close to the nose of a hungry conger.

If it is sizeable and gets a scent of the bait it will move partly out of its hole, just far enough to grab the bait. As you

strike, your first task is to get the conger out of its lair and into the midwater where you can play it – it can be a dire tug-of-war business and if the tackle is not strong enough the conger will surely win.

Fish such as codling, whiting, and pouting are likely to be around the pier supports where they find plenty of natural food growing on or living in the weed-covered structures, and this is supplemented by edible food items

Above: *A steeply-sloping shore provides an opportunity to reach deep water without long casting.*

Below: *Stone breakwaters provide convenient platforms for anglers who prefer to do their deepwater fishing from dry land, and attract a wide variety of fish. They feed among the rocks and the seaweeds on the stonework, and some, such as conger, may live in crevices.*

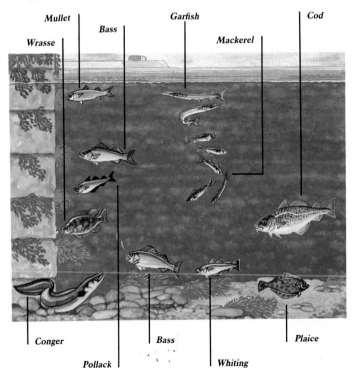

Mullet
Wrasse
Bass
Garfish
Mackerel
Cod

Conger
Pollack
Bass
Whiting
Plaice

thrown or dropped by visitors. These often attract bass, mullet and garfish right under the fisherman's platform.

Where cafés or restaurants have premises on piers, the unwanted food scraps jettisoned into the sea also ensure a plentiful food supply for fish. But keep the bait off the bottom; the food supply attracts hordes of nuisance crabs which tear at baits when they are legered.

Many piers and breakwaters can only be fished from after payment of a fee, so make sure you arrive with the necessary coinage. Local authorities also establish bylaws concerning fishing; these are usually exhibited near the entrance to the pier.

HARBOURS

A harbour offers a variety of fishing possibilities: it may be frequented by a number of species and there are usually many areas of fairly deep water. Visits must be carefully timed, however, during the holiday season, because the activities of holidaymakers tend to keep fish away.

There is no need for long casting, but it is not wise simply to lower the

Below: *Stormy weather which could ruin a fishing trip in an open boat does not worry the anglers on this harbour breakwater.*

tackle straight down off the wall or pier. Rocks and all kinds of rubbish accumulate there and the terminal tackle can quickly become lodged.

Where commercial boats are moored, especially fishing trawlers, mullet cruise around waiting for food scraps. These areas often have some resident conger, free-swimming bass and pollack which have been conditioned to find food there.

The long concrete breakwaters that extend out to the entrance of some harbours make very good fishing platforms. They give access to the water inside the harbour and also, from the other side, allow fishing in the open sea. These solid structures often have rock-strewn sides covered with kelp – they are ideal holding spots for conger. Mullet are also attracted by the food among the kelp.

If night fishing is allowed, then assuming the tide is right, harbours can offer fine fishing. But always stay aware of the deep water at your feet; a harbour on a dark night can be a very dangerous place.

SANDBANKS

Tidal action causes sandbanks, which are found in various places, from estuaries to deep, offshore areas. All sandbanks hold fish, particularly bass, turbot, plaice, brill and dabs

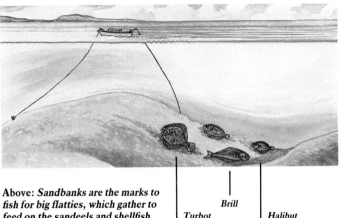

Above: Sandbanks are the marks to fish for big flatties, which gather to feed on the sandeels and shellfish.

Turbot | Brill | Halibut

which feed on the sandeel population.

Alongside the sandeels there are razorshells, cockles, crabs and sprats. All this natural food attracts fish, the location of the sandbank controlling the species. In some areas tope visit sandbanks, preying on the other fish feeding there.

Sandbanks very in depth, with holes and deeper channels where dogfish, rays and whiting can be

Below: Although the landing net is ready, this turbot hooked from a sandbank off the Cornish coast is still playing hard to get.

contacted. Flatfish also lie in the channels through the banks waiting for the making tide to bring food along in the form of sprats and fish fry.

Boat fishing over sandbanks can be carried out on the drift or while at anchor. Drifting covers a lot of ground and it offers the opportunity to present a bait in a natural way, flowing with other food items in the tidal current.

A fairly strong tide is the best time to fish these places, but during the very powerful spring tides fishing can be difficult, almost impossible from a drifting boat owing to the speed with which it is taken over the banks.

ROUGH GROUND

The nature of the seabed varies enormously, from flat mud and sand to hard, chalky surfaces and banks of stones. Patches of rough ground, broken by stones, rocks, coarse sand, depressions and undulations, attract a variety of natural food for fish, including crabs, mussels, limpets, winkles, whelks, hermit crabs, peeler and soft crabs, as well as many small fish and marine worms. All these attract quality fish.

Shoals of bream spend part of their season over these areas, packs of tope and smooth hound hunt there, and the occasional big skate glides in to feed.

There are usually a few clear patches of sand dotted about rough ground, and flatfish settle there. Even big pollack leave the reefs to rove over rough ground, and conger in the 20lb (9kg) range explore these places.

When fishing with a running leger, it is a wise precaution to attach the weight by a length of weaker line – a rotten-bottom – or fish the bait just off the seabed to avoid snagging. These risks are worth taking, however, because rough ground marks are capable of providing a great day's fishing. If the tide is right, a drift

Above: *Strong tackle is needed for reef fishing. Here a powerful boat rod bends steeply as a pollack drives for the security of the rocks.*

across such an area using a pirk or baited feathers can bring in a mixed bag of really good fish.

REEFS

The inshore and offshore reefs which are marked on marine charts as potential dangers to shipping are excellent fishing marks. Their caverns, canyons, gullies and plateaux hold many of the best sporting species, and big pollack, bream, bass, cod, ling and conger, all running to real specimen weight, are found over, in and at the foot of the reef.

Conger and ling usually lurk deep in the heart of the reef, and techniques similar to those used in wreck fishing must be employed to get the fish away from their lairs and into open water. The rods used must be capable of fishing 25-30lb (11-13.6kg) b.s. line, and numerous breakages can make reef congering an expensive business. A minimum of a dozen 100lb (45kg) b.s. wire traces, plus heavy-duty weights and trace accessories, is normally carried by serious reef conger anglers.

Pollack, bass and cod are generally found over and around the reef, and line of 12-17lb (5.4-7.7kg) b.s. is quite adequate. Redgill or Eddystone lures can prove deadly at these marks, fished on long flowing traces which can also be used to present king rag, live sandeel or mackerel strip in an attractive manner.

The flowing trace should be allowed to stream out in the tide before the weight and boom are lowered into the water – this avoids a tangle as the line is gently dropped down. As the weight touches the seabed, reel in quickly for a few turns, then retrieve the tackle slowly,

counting the turns of the handle. This will enable you to assess the depth at which the fish are feeding when you get the first bite. At the next drop you will know where to put the bait.

A bite on one of these long traces is rarely felt, the fish usually signalling its presence by a slow pull. If the hook does not set home on the first strike, continue the retrieve – the fish will often attack the bait a second time.

WRECKS

The waters round northern Europe are dotted with the wrecks of ships. Some, such as the *Lusitania*, are well-known beyond angling and nautical circles, but most are the remains of humble ships lost in heavy weather or on reefs, or sunk by enemy action during wartime. All have become the homes of fish, and some of these fish are very large indeed.

A sunken ship rapidly becomes little more than a reef, containing

Below: *The varied underwater terrain of a reef offers food and security to all types of fish; reefs are among the most productive of sea angling marks.*

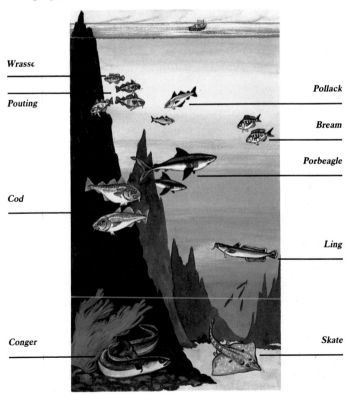

Wrasse

Pollack

Pouting

Bream

Porbeagle

Cod

Ling

Conger

Skate

plenty of places where fish can live. The holds, superstructures and cabins all offer shelter.

Finding a wreck has become relatively easy owing to the development of sophisticated echo-sounding and radio navigation equipment. Now charterboats and even private craft can pinpoint wrecks with confidence, and wreck-fishing has become one of the most popular aspects of the sport.

Having located a wreck, the skipper will use his knowledge of the tide to position the boat so that all the anglers on board can fish their baits close to it, either anchoring or, if appropriate, drifting with the tide along the length of the sunken ship.

It is not unusual to need 2lb (0.9kg) of lead to get the bait as close to the wreck as possible. Conger are the target inside the structure itself, and a well-established wreck may hold a number of really weighty specimens. There is no mistaking the bite of such a fish: a sudden reaction on the line, then a slow withdrawal as the conger

Right: *Many wrecks have become homes for specimen conger and ling, and also attract other big fish such as cod, pollack and coalfish.*

Below: *This party of club anglers are well pleased with their catch of conger and ling, taken from a wreck in the English Channel.*

Cod

Pollack and Coalfish

Ling

Black and Red Bream

Turbot

Conger

backs towards its lair. This must be stopped at all costs, since once a big conger is back inside a wreck the angler may as well cut his line as try to pull it out. It is essential to get the fish off the bottom quickly, even at the risk of breaking the line; once it is in open water you have a chance of pumping it to the surface.

Outside the wreck, but still within its shelter, are turbot, anglerfish, red and black bream. A simple two-hook paternoster is a good rig for red bream, although few wreck-fishermen actively seek them. Record-sized turbot are certainly worth going for, however, and there is always the chance of hooking an angler fish.

Close to the surface of the wreck there are often ling, while higher up will be pollack and coalfish. Drift fishing is usually the best way of contacting these fish, using rapidly-retrieved rubber eels as lures. The

Above: *Hauling a big fish from the depths of a wreck mark can put a big strain on the tackle – breakages are inevitable.*

best pattern is normally the Redgill Wrecker, but on some heavily-fished wrecks the fish may be more likely to take an Eddystone Eel.

Wrecking tackle

Wreck fishing can be great sport, but it is tough and rough on both the angler and the tackle. An ideal wrecking outfit is a 50lb (22.6kg) class rod with a Penn Senator 6/0 reel, or a Tatler IV, loaded with 50lb or even 60lb (27kg) b.s. line. Traces are best made of 100lb (45kg) b.s. nylon, which is more pliable than wire and does not need special rod fittings. Most wreck fish have plenty of teeth, but with the exception of conger they will not sever heavy-duty nylon.

TECHNIQUES

BEACHCASTING

With the help of a good teacher, raw beginners can cast 100 yards (90m) within a day of first picking up a beachcaster. You can teach youself, of course, but it will take longer and may create bad habits.

Beach tackle

Today, even the cheapest tackle offers reasonable casting power. Forget about special blanks, tuned reels and advanced tournament techniques if all you want to do is cast 120 yards (109m) or so. A medium-fast 5oz (140g) rod, about 12ft (3.6m) long, a small multiplier with brake blocks or magnetic casting control, a 15lb (6.8kg) b.s. reel line and 40-50lb (18-22.6kg) b.s. leader to take the shock of the cast, makes up a well-matched outfit for most situations.

How to do it

Long casting is achieved by the body and tackle working efficiently together. Above all, the system that must be learned allows the rod to work properly, and this means transferring the power through the rod sections, down the line and into the weight.

Above: *A long caster in action. The power of the cast – probably well over 150 yards (137m) – can be seen in the bend of the rod.*

On the beach, stand facing the water with your feet shoulder-width apart and angled (see diagram). Select the place where the lead is intended to

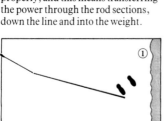

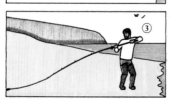

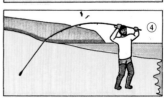

Left and above: *The casting sequence:* ① *Place the feet properly.* ② *Lay the tackle back on the ground.* ③ *Pull the rod forward.* ④ *Punch the rod up with one hand while pulling the butt down with the other.* ⑤ *Aim high in the air and release the line as the weight flies forward. Take care when casting to check no-one is in the way.*

go. It must travel towards an imaginary target at about 45 degrees.

Height is absolutely essential to good casting. If you just aim at a spot on the water the cast will tend to go low and left, because the whole line of the power flow is wrong.

Let the weight hang about 5ft 91.5m) below the rod tip and make the reel ready for casting. Make sure there is no one behind you, then swivel round from the water and toss the weight on to the beach with rod and leader fully extended in a straight line.

The rod tip must be low, no more than 6in (15cm) from the beach, with your right arm held comfortably stretched away from the water, and your left hand slightly to the left of your face and about a foot (30cm) from the shoulder. The position of your left elbow is important – it must be held high, at shoulder level.

Forget the technicalities – turn your head to look up at the aiming point, and pull the rod forward in a spear-throwing action. It must be done smoothly and positively, but not very powerfully. This will develop in time. As the rod slides forward, your left hand rises and extends, and your right moves in a punching motion, with the elbow bent.

Nothing much will seem to happen to the rod, but it is actually beginning to bend, and the weight is accelerating. Speed up the sequence by driving your right hand upwards and forwards, while pulling your left hand down to the bottom left of your ribs. The result is a powerful, flowing punch-pull action that terminates in line release.

Momentum of the rod and body will put you into a natural follow-through position in which the rod tip points towards the aiming mark in the sky. You will see the weight fly into your line of sight, and all you have to do is watch its trajectory, first to check that it is high and straight, and secondly to decide when to stop the line running off the spool.

Multipliers must be braked immediately the weight hits the water, otherwise a monumental bird's nest will form in an instant. Fixed-spool reels may also need controlling, for

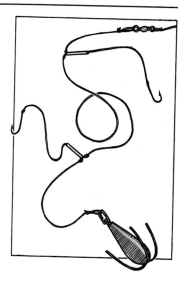

Above: *A basic paternoster rig for beach fishing. The snoods are linked to stand-off loops stiffened with lengths of plastic tubing.*

they can backlash to some extent when the spool is loaded with light line.

The first cast may feel awkward and even uncomfortable; you must relax, think the action through, and try again. Eventually it will get easier.

Terminal rigs

Rigs can be as simple or as complex as you want. Fish are not aware of whether they are faced with a simple rig or an elaborate arrangement of beads, swivels and booms. What can affect them is the way the bait is presented.

Leger tackle is used by at least 90 per cent of all shore anglers. There are two important rigs: the multi-hook paternoster and the single-hook rig which is an updated version of the traditional running leger. In their simplest forms both rigs are easy to tie and very reliable. They also cast well and catch plenty of fish.

Which rig to use depends on the fishing available. Two- and three-hook paternosters are the choice for whiting, dab, flounder, eel and school bass. These and similar species take small baits, so fine wire hooks, size 4-1, are adequate.

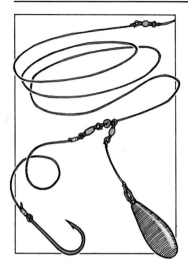

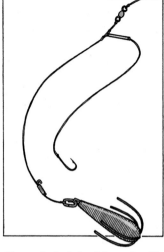

Above: *A tope or conger rig: the hook is crimped to 24in (60cm) of cable-laid wire which is linked to a heavy nylon trace.*

Above: *A single-hook leger rig with bait clip for big cod or bass. The hook length is attached to a stiffened stand-off loop.*

Light nylon snoods of 12-20lb (5.4-9kg) b.s. combine excellent presentation with ample b.s. for landing the fish. The exact design of the rig is unimportant, and most anglers develop their own favourites. There are no real rules about what is best, so experiment with lines of different b.s., hook sizes and dimensions, to find a rig that suits.

Big fish such as cod, large bass and dogfish prefer a generous bite of bait on a reasonably long trace of about 30in (75cm). There should be no more than a single hook because long-distance casting is virtually impossible with more, and on most beaches long-distance casting is the key to success.

Use tough, forged steel hooks in the 1/0-8/0 bracket, tied to 20-35lb (9-16kg) b.s. nylon. A bait clip just above the rig streamlines the baited hook throughout the cast and releases it when the tackle hits the water.

Big tope and conger chew through the strongest nylon traces, but not through cable-laid wire. These are the only shore-caught species that demand such robust terminal rigs. High-quality stainless wire between 50-100lb (22.6-45.3kg) b.s. should be

used, crimped to a hook such as the Mustad Seamaster.

Extra swivels along the line are worthwhile because tope and conger often spin when being played. The slightest kink can reduce the b.s. of the wire by half.

Tope will also roll on the tackle and snap the line with their very powerful and abrasive tails. You can guard againt this by linking the trace to the reel line with a 3-6ft (1-2m) length of 50lb (22.6kg) b.s. nylon.

FLOAT FISHING

Float fishing is not as prevalent in sea fishing as it is in freshwater. A great deal of sea fishing is done in considerable depths of water, of over 200ft (180m), and unless fish are known to be present in the upper layers float-fishing would be a waste of time. Most sea fish feed on or near the bottom of the sea.

Then there is the question of wave action: for a float to be effective it must register bites when a fish takes the bait, but on a choppy sea, which is usually accompanied by a brisk wind, any float would be so knocked about that a bite could go unnoticed.

There are times, however, when float technique is not only possible but preferred. The species that can be caught on a float-fished rig at sea include bass, wrasse, mackerel and of course shark. In shark fishing, the float is used mainly as a buoy. It does, however, support the large fishbait somewhere in midwater and therefore it is true float fishing.

Float technique can be practised in the quiet waters of a harbour, basin, or enclosed bay; sometimes very still areas of water can be found among rocks. Here, the float will support the bait and keep the tackle clear of weed and kelp beds, which would soon snag a legered rig.

Slider float

There are many occasions when the depth the bait must be fished at is much greater than the length of the rod. If the float is fixed and the bait is being fished at, say 20ft (6m), the baited hook must be lowered over the side of the boat or harbour wall before the float is attached. This will be all right until the time comes to reel in. Then, when the float is reached, it will jam into the tip ring, leaving 20ft of line still in the water.

This is where the slider float comes into its own. This useful item of gear runs freely on the line, so that when the tackle is cast out the float sits on the water while the line passes through it. When the required depth is reached the float comes up against a stop which has been placed on the line, supporting the rig at the required depth. proper retrieval is possible too, as line just runs through the rings on the float freely, allowing the terminal tackle to be drawn right up.

The slider float also enables long casts to be made from piers and harbour walls. The terminal tackle stays compact until it reaches the water, and the weight then pulls the baited hook down, leaving the float on the surface to act as a bite indicator.

Right: *A shark angler attaches balloon floats to the line using thin thread. When a shark takes the bait the thread snaps and the floats drift clear, out of the way.*

DRIFT-LINE FISHING

This method uses a simple rig consisting of a weight and a swivel connecting the reel line to a 4-6ft (1.2-1.8m) nylon trace with a baited hook or lure. Live sandeel is an ideal bait.

The rig is allowed to drift on the tide, the strength of which dictates the weight needed to take the bait down to the fish. If the tide is really slack, all weight can be removed, allowing the rig to sink under the weight of the bait.

A light rod can be used, for there is no casting to be done, but if a big fish is contacted the angler will need all his skill to bring it to the boat. Whatever the rod used, the reel – a centre-pin, fixed-spool or multiplier – must have sufficient capacity to hold a lot of line.

This tackle can be drifted in close to rocks, where wrasse come upon it as it swirls in the eddies. If the wind and tide are in the right place, drift-lining can also be used to good effect from piers or jetties.

Below: *The leger weight may be linked to the rig by a 'rotten bottom' of weak nylon; if it snags, a sharp tug on the line snaps the link, and only the weight is lost.*

Above: *This angler has hooked a conger while fishing from a stone and concrete harbour wall – a snaggy mark well suited to 'rotten bottom' tackle.*

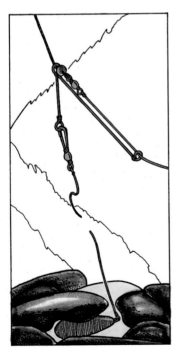

PATERNOSTERING

Basically, a paternoster rig is one which has the weight at the bottom of the line, and the hook or hooks on snoods of nylon or on booms of wire or plastic, projecting from the reel line. This kind of rig is useful for catching many species of fish. The usual arrangement for boat or pier fishing is a three-hook rig; beachcasters seldom use anything other than a single hook because the complexity of more than one tends to restrict casting distance.

The snoods can be attached to the nylon trace by two-loop connections, or the loops can be paternostered on wire or plastic of various lengths. The snoods should be fitted far enough apart on the trace to prevent them from tangling with the one above or below. The lower hook snood should be the longest, while the next one up should be shorter so that it does not touch the lower one. Take care not to mount the top snood too high up the line, for it can tangle at the rod tip when you are reeling in a fish which has been hooked on the bottom snood.

Above: *Paternoster leger tackle is often used by boat anglers to fish a bait for bottom-feeding species while the paternostered baits attract fish feeding in midwater.*

When paternostering from a boat the weight should be just enough to hold bottom, the reel line from rod tip to tackle being kept taut while the hooks stream out in the tide. If the weight is right, the rod tip can be raised occasionally and a few feet of line let out, allowing the tackle to drop downtide a short distance so that the area is searched.

The hooks can be baited with a variety of items, such as strips of mackerel, worms, squid, crab, and shellfish. Most species will take a paternostered bait when they come upon one.

Paternoster leger

The combination of a leger rig and paternoster is popular with boat anglers. In this rig the weight is connected by a Clement's boom and from this a flowing trace legers a bait on the bottom. Above the weight, one or two hooks are paternostered. This rig has the big advantage of taking middle-water fish as well as the bottom-feeding species.

LEGERING

When the two hooks from up the trace are removed, the bottom hook can be left to leger on the seabed. In a strong tide the hook trace can be any length up to 25ft (7.6m) when fishing for bottom-hugging species such as turbot and the various rays. A trace of 6ft (1.8m) or longer is known as a flowing trace. The baited hook on the end is swirled about in the current, bringing it to the attention of searching fish.

When legering, the weight can be attached by a clip-swivel, Kilmore boom or a Clement's boom, the latter being the most widely used. This boom allows the line to run freely when a fish picks up the bait and because there is no resistance the fish take is more certain.

Cod anglers usually fish leger-wise with a single hook on a 20ft (6m) trace, but anglers seeking smaller fish such as whiting, pouting and dogfish rig up a two- or three-hook trace. Sea match anglers favour the multi-hook rig, and use different baits on each hook, hoping to take two or three fish at a time to build up a winning weight.

When the tide slackens, knowing anglers switch from the leger to the paternoster, simply by adding one or two hooks above the weight.

UPTIDE CASTING

Until a few years ago, boat anglers at anchor would sit at the stern, and cast or simply release the tackle to be taken downtide – eventually, according to the weight used, settling on the seabed. But an intriguing style has now evolved called uptide casting, the tackle being cast from the bows up-tide and away from the boat.

The method works best when the boat is anchored over a sandbank or close to the shore in shallow water, or in an estuary. The theory behind uptide casting is based on the fact that the vessel moored in the tide-race creates a V-shaped area of disturbed water which discourages fish from coming near. Even the anchor rope, running away from the bows uptide, gives rise to turbulence. The vibration and noise created by anglers moving about in the boat can also disturb the fish. For these reasons it is best if the terminal tackle is presented to the fish before they reach the area of the anchor rope or the boat itself. This is what uptide casting achieves.

Tackle

A fast-taper rod of 8-10ft (2.4-3m) with standard rings and fittings is the best to use. As an alternative, a beachcasting rod can be used, with the butt end cut down to a manageable length for the confined area of a boat.

The reel, a multiplier or fixed-spool according to choice, should be loaded

Below: **Uptide casting places the rig well clear of the turbulence caused by the anchored boat. When a fish takes, the lead pulls free.**

with line of about 15lb (6.8kg) b.s. – but select line of the finest diameter possible to cut down the drag. The casting weight should be from 3oz to 5oz (85-140g) depending on the tide, but as usual always use the lightest possible. A grapnel lead with long wires will hold the bait in position up and away from the boat, and the breakaway pattern is preferable.

Casting the bait

To make the cast, the rod should be brought parallel to the side of the boat. Never swing the weight and the baited hook inboard, and always warn the other occupants of the boat before casting. With the rod pointing downtide, over the side of the boat, the tackle is cast up and away uptide. It is important to give extra slack line as soon as the weight is in the sea, allowing as much as 20-25 yards (18-23m) of line to run off. The tide will take the weight to the bottom and then the grip-wires dig into the seabed.

If slack line is not given, the lead will drift downtide and across other lines, causing tangles and disrupting the fishing. When the lead is held fast by the grip-wires the tide will pull the rod-tip over into an arc, so the rod should be held or tied fast. If just stood to rest on the side it will topple.

Fish that hunt for food in the tide do not nudge the bait. Bass, dogfish, cod and whiting tend to snatch and such bites are registered by the rod tip springing back as a fish picks up the bait, this in turn lifting the lead off the seabed. The grip-wires are pulled out of the sand or mud and the rod tip bounces back.

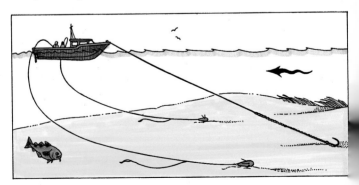

A strike is not necessary – just reel in as fast as possible to take up all the slack line until the fish is contacted; the rod is lifted high and the fish is on. Hooked uptide, the fish is fought down with the current to the boat.

Above: *A trolling rod in action, fitted into a rod-socket attached to the boat. A safety-line tied to the rail guards against possible loss of the equipment.*

TROLLING

Trolling is simply towing a bait or lure behind a moving boat. If the boat is moving slowly enough, anglers sometimes tow a spinner or feathers in order to catch mackerel for bait while on their way out to the fishing area. But serious trolling is a method of catching bass, pollack, and occasionally porbeagle and halibut.

Natural baits and artificial lures are used, the natural baits being mackerel, sprat, sandeel and long thin strips of large squid. The size of hook depends upon the size of the bait, but generally they range from 1/0 to 6/0. The hook is attached to a trace about

18-20ft (5.4-6m) long and depending on the depth the bait can be trolled up to 100 yards (90m) behind the boat.

A comfortable boat speed should be settled upon, and the weight selected to troll at the required water level. The Jardine spinning lead is the best weight to use. Available in a range of sizes, it has brass wire spirals at each end, and can be mounted on the line at any time; the line is woven between the spirals to hold the lead firm wherever the angler decides. Two can be used if necessary. If the Jardine is bent into a half-moon shape it becomes an anti-kink lead, and when used with swivels its prevents much of the nuisance of line twist.

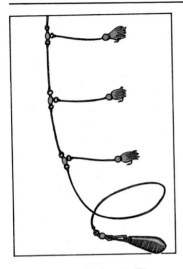

Above: *A basic jigging rig. The lures are linked to three-way swivels, while the lead weight is attached by a quick-release clip.*

Above: *Jigging a string of feathers from a boat on the way to a mark is a very effective way of catching mackerel for use as bait.*

JIGGING

Jigging, or pirking, is a deepwater method of fishing for pollack, coalfish, cod and ling. In general, jigging is done with small artificial lures, made of metal and feathers. Some jigs have the added attraction of a few coloured plastic strips, and look like plastic squid; others look like red rubber eels. Most jigs can have fish strips attached to the hooks as an additional attraction.

Most jigs are fished three at a time and a basic rig is for each to be paternostered on a short snood attached to a three-way swivel. A lead weight is needed to take the rig down.

Pirks are much heavier lures, designed to be fished in very deep water, usually from a drifting boat.

Above: *Jigging can be a good technique for bigger fish, too. Here a cod is unhooked from a rubber eel which was jigged from a boat drifting over a deepwater mark.*

Some pirks may be as heavy as 2lb (0.9kg). The weight of the pirk depends on the depth of water to be fished, a heavy one getting down faster. It is important to mount a large multiplier reel on the rod, with the capacity to hold 100 yards (90m) of 50lb (22.6kg) nylon.

Methods

There are different ways to fish pirks and jigs. Some anglers allow the lure to make a controlled drop to a certain level before letting it go further.

Various levels may be tried both on the way down and the way up. Sometimes when the fish are found the angler finds himself struggling with three big pollack or coalfish hooked on the lures!

Another method, used mainly with the pirk, is to cast it well away from the boat and allow it to sink towards the bottom. It may be taken by a fish either on the way down or during the retrieval. Jigging and pirking continues through the length of each drift, each angler usually alternating between baited and unbaited lures. At the end of the drift the tackle is reeled in while the craft heads back to start another drift.

The same jigging action is employed when fishing with feathered and baited hooks. Feathering is normally associated with mackerel fishing, often for the purposes of gathering sufficient fish for a day's bottom fishing. Mackerel feathers consist of six feathered hooks paternoster-rigged up the trace. A lead weight is fitted to the extreme end and at the other a quick-release swivel allows the trace to be attached to the reel line.

This tackle is lowered or cast out by the under-arm method, and allowed to sink. It is important not to let it all hit the seabed and come to rest in a pile. The hooks are liable to catch in each other and you will finally retrieve a matted, entangled mess. Feel carefully for the seabed, and when the weight touches, stop instantly. The reel should be wound up a few turns, then the rod tip raised and lowered. At the other end, this creates an impression of six small fish moving up and down in the tide – a tasty morsel for feeding mackerel.

This sink-and-draw movement should be continued at different depths, and when fish take the bite is easily felt. Often as the feathers are drawn through a mackerel shoal several will be hooked at the same time and as they all try to swim in different directions the effect on the angler playing them is dramatic.

Other species can be taken on feathered hooks, and for this a three-hook rig is used, normally fitted with larger hooks, although the smaller mackerel feathers are ideal for bream. The larger ones are used for cod and pollack. Feathered hooks may be fished baited and unbaited.

Below: *A selection of jigging lures and pirks: ① Artificial squid, with feathered hook. ② A big chrome-plated pirk, with a treble hook. ③ A small pirk, shaped to resemble a fish. ④ and ⑤ Rubber imitation sandeels of the Redgill type. ⑥ Mackerel spinner. ⑦ A heavy pirk for deepwater fishing, fitted with heavy-duty swivels.*

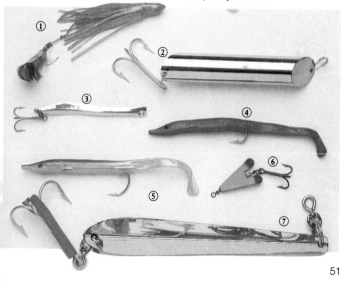

COD *Gadus morhua*

Waters: Offshore and inshore marks, over clean and rough ground; steep, shelving beaches, occasionally near deepwater wrecks and reefs.
Baits: Lugworm, sprat, sandeel, squid, cuttlefish, mussel, peeler and soft crab, artificial lures, feathers.
Techniques: Leger, paternoster, sink-and-draw, pirking, baited feathers.

The cod is one of the most common European sea fish. It has three dorsal fins along its mottled, green-brown back, an arched lateral line, and a long chin barbel. Reaching near 100lb (45kg), with rod-caught specimens recorded in the 50lb (23kg) mark, and in demand as a table fish, the cod is a prime target for anglers.

Until they reach some 5lb (2.2kg) in weight, the species is known as codling. In the southern European waters the cod is a winter species, but in northern waters they provide all-year-round sport, and although prolific they tend to be smaller on average than those taken in the south. In the Orkney area, numbers of cod can be taken between 3 and 8lb (1.3-3.6kg), with fish of 15lb (6.8kg) regarded as large for the area, whereas in the south a cod of this size is hardly worth a mention.

This fish is a favourite quarry for all sea anglers whether they fish from the shore or a boat.

When boat fishing for cod, it is important to take into account the size of fish to be expected when choosing tackle; the strength of tide and the depth of water must also be considered. For boat fishing off the south coast of Britain, where big cod are fairly common, a rod of 30-50lb (13-23kg) class is needed, which may be thought of as heavy gear. But when a big cod is hooked in a strong tide its first struggles are very powerful, and coupled with the effects of the huge gaping mouth acting as an extra brake the fight can be severe.

Ideally the rod should incorporate a high quality tip roller ring in order that wire line can be used. The best rods for wire use have a full set of roller rings, but a single one will often suffice. Recommended reels are the Penn Senator 4/0 or 6/0, the Penn Super Mariner, or a Tatler III or IV.

When fishing waters where the cod run small, the same reels should be used, but rods of the 20-30lb (9-13kg) class substituted. Lines are a matter of choice, but it pays to carry a reel loaded with 40lb (18kg) b.s. nylon and another with 40lb b.s. wire, which can be single or multi-strand.

Above: *Uptide casting over a shallow mark, with a strong tide, led to the capture of this 20lb (9kg) cod.*

Fishing techniques for cod vary a great deal from one area to another. Off Scotland and Ireland, where the water is clear and the fish numerous, many anglers use feathers, white being the traditional colour.

Another effective cod lure which is most attractive when used in deepwater is the pirk. This comes in a variety of weights, usually with a large treble hook attached. However, this treble has a tendency to foul-hook too many fish and the sporting angler often removes it and substitutes a 8/0 or 10/0 single hook. Pirk fishing is a non-stop work, but it does produce good catches.

Below: *Prized by anglers as a large and highly edible fish, the cod's large head and capacious mouth make it easily identifiable.*

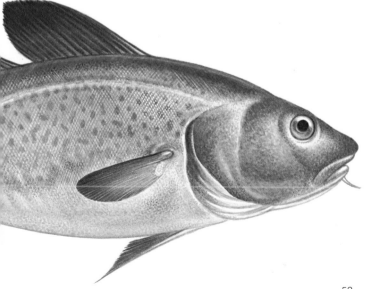

The shore angler's season for cod is limited to the winter months in most areas. As the water warms in late spring, it seems that the cod fall back into the preferred cold depths. The exceptions are the coasts of north-east England and Scotland, where codling can be caught from the shore throughout the summer months. But the farther south one goes the harder it is to find good inshore cod when the sun warms the water. There is an early spring migration to spawning grounds in northern latitudes, with some large specimens staying in the deep waters to the south.

Although the cod has not achieved fame for its fighting qualities it does provide a considerable challenge to the inshore angler because of its sheer weight and size. Hauling a large cod inshore through a tangle of weed and against the winter waves demands strong muscles and resilient tackle.

Not all shore-caught cod are small. At least one fish well over 40lb (18kg) has been taken from a Welsh coast shore, and many 20lb (9kg) fish.

The cod is a bottom feeder and will take all the usual baits. Strangely, most cod when boated are full of different food than that which tempted them. Their large mouths can engulf large food items; a cod of 7lb (3kg) can easily take a whiting of 1lb (0.45kg), which is an indication of the fact that large baits are essential.

Locating cod from the shore during the winter months is less of a problem than it may appear to be. Experienced anglers know the best cod beaches and the appearance of cod can be forecast very accurately every year at the same places round the coast.

The differences between venues generally relate to the size of the fish most commonly caught in specific areas, rocky marks being more suitable for the smaller codling because of the limited food supply. The bigger cod favour the open beaches where large shoals of small whiting, herring and sprat can be preyed upon.

As with most fish species, the smaller cod and codling are found in larger numbers, while the very large specimens are usually solitary, their huge appetites keeping them constantly on the move.

The large shoals are of course steadily depleted by commercial fishing, and as the fish become larger their numbers decrease. This leads to separate shoals of fish moving round the coast, each having fish of about the same age and size.

Sometimes these shoals become mixed, codling and large specimens sharing the same feeding grounds. For this reason, specimen-hunting

Below: The double-hook rig is ideal for the beach. A baitclip (inset) holds the bait in place, streamlining the rig for casting, while two hooks increase catching power.

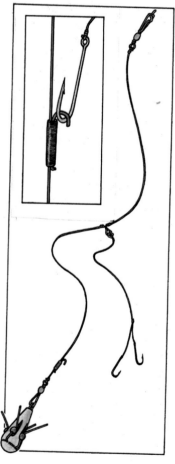

Above: *The angler had to cast well out from the beach to capture these two fine cod. They fell to a classic cod bait of peeler crab.*

tactics are not necessary. A short session at a known peak time can often produce better results than long marathons.

Tackle must be robust at all times, since one never knows when something out of the ordinary will be hooked. This makes hauling a codling up on a rod, line and reel capable of controlling a 40lb (18kg) specimen something of an anticlimax, but better that than suddenly finding that you are struggling to cope with a fish which is likely to break either your rod or your line.

Because of their fast growth rate and voracious appetite cod are continuously in search of food and become great opportunists when a prolific food source is provided by weather conditions. Gales which scour worms and shellfish from the seabed and wash them inshore can be a boon to anglers. Some of the best catches have been made during or following onshore gales. Darkness and disturbed, coloured water provide cod with cover and tempt them to probe close to the shore. This is when the beach-angler's chances of a big cod are good. The spring tides often create such conditions, with fish activity at a peak. Waiting for times such as these and then fishing the incoming tide is better than making haphazard trips to the shore in the hope of a lucky codling or two.

BASS *Dicentrarchus labrax*

Waters: Offshore sandbanks, reefs, surf beaches, rocky headlands, estuaries, harbours, creeks.
Baits: Peeler and soft crab, hermit crab, sandeel, lugworm, ragworm, prawn, slipper limpet, razorfish, squid, pirks and other artificial lures.
Techniques: Free-lining, spinning, drift lining, running leger, trolling, paternoster, float fishing.

The bass is a species related to the perch, part of the large group of spiny fishes. It has two dorsal fins, the first carrying several sharp spines, which also appear on the gill covers. The back of the fish is a greenish-grey shading to a metallic blue-grey, with flanks of bright silver and a silvery-white belly. Being a predator it feeds on small fish and other live animals. Bass reach at least 20lb (9kg), but any bass over 10lb (4.5kg) is a worthy catch. The average is about 3-4lb (1.3-1.8kg), smaller ones being known as school bass.

This fish is keenly sought by many anglers, both for its table qualities and its fighting ability when hooked on light tackle. Small bass remain inshore throughout the year, bigger bass coming in with the tide to follow the breakers which disturb marine worms and other life for the fish to snap up. They also feed over mudflats and sandbanks in sandy bays. Shoals of brit and other small fish are preyed upon by roving bass, the surface being disturbed as the small fish scatter.

Small bass remain in areas where there may be warm water from power-station outflows. They keep together, feeding and scavenging along the bottom, and occasionally rising to the surface.

These shoals move round pier supports, wooden piles, jetties, rocks and patches of weed searching for food. Where there are storm beaches, with breakers to rough up the seabed, they follow the incoming tide feeding on animal food swirling about in the disturbed water. They also feed freely at night, particularly in the summer when many beaches are occupied by holiday-makers during the day, many of whom leave edible matter on the sand at low water, to be picked up by the fish as the tide rises.

The tackle needed for bass varies with the techniques. When bass fishing from a boat the best rod is a light 9-10ft (2.7-3m) model, or 12lb (5.4kg) class rod with a matching line

Above: *A combination bait of peeler crab and squid tempted this good average bass, caught from the beach at Reculver on the Channel.*

Below: *One of the great sporting fish, the spiky bass needs careful handling. There is a close relative, the spotted bass.*

of 10-12lb (4.5-5.4kg) b.s. The reel can be a multiplier, fixed-spool or centrepin. For hooks, use 1/0 to 4/0 according to the size of bait.

Shore anglers can use a fairly long rod because of the distance needed to cast out, suitable for line of 15-20lb (6.8-9kg) b.s. This increase in b.s. is due to the wear and tear put on line when it is used close to sand. The reel should be a multiplier or fixed-spool. For casting, weights of 4-6oz (113-170g) are used, while the most popular baits are crab and ragworm.

Peeler crab has accounted for a great many bass, and it is the favourite of many regular bass anglers. A size 2/0 hook is generally used and the crab is prepared by removing the legs and much of the hard shell without damaging the soft body. This bait is held on the hook by the use of elastic thread, making sure that the point is left exposed. The thread helps the soft bait to stay on the hook during the cast and as it is rolled about on the seabed.

Long-distance casting is not always needed for bass because they often feed quite close in.

Another effective method is float fishing, particularly from a boat, but the same style can be used from piers, rocks, or any projection that allows angling. Where bass are known to be

Above: _Long-distance casting for bass is not necessary from beaches such as this one in Kent. The fish are often found close inshore._

present, great sport can be had by free-lining a live sandeel in the tide.

Drifting over an offshore sandbank with light tackle has also accounted for high-quality bass. It is done with a 12lb (5.4kg) class outfit, a long, flowing trace of 15-20ft (4.5-6m) and a sandeel. It is important to use the slow drift and the long trace to give a free and natural movement to the bait. The sandeel should be mounted on a size 1/0 or 2/0 long-shanked hook and kept down by a 2oz (60g) bored lead bullet running free on the line. The idea is to keep the bait moving on the seabed. There will be no mistaking the bite when a bass takes the bait, for the rod top dips suddenly.

As many as two or three fine bass can be taken on each drift during this exciting form of fishing, each giving the angler an entertaining tussle.

Occasionally a large shoal will be encountered and the effect of their attacks on surface brit is dramatic, the sea breaking into spray as the small fish try to flee. This disturbance also attracts sea birds, which cash in on the activity to take their share of the shoal.

It is the sight of gulls weaving and diving in a confined area that often alerts the angler to bass.

One method of taking bass at these times is to use spinning tackle, especially from a boat, although it can be done if the shore angler is at or near water level. Spinning cannot be accomplished properly if the angler is too high to work the spinner correctly.

The bright, flashy spinner, worked through the brit mass, imitates one of the small fish. When it is taken by a bass in full attack the result is spectacular and rewarding.

Below: *Three fine bass caught on live sandeel fished on 12lb (5.4kg) gear, from the famous Skerries Bank off the Devon coast.*

MULLET

Waters: Shallow coastal waters such as sheltered beaches, harbours, estuaries, piers, docks, brackish waters in marshland creeks, tidal reaches of rivers.

Baits: Bread, maggot, redworm, small harbour ragworm, shrimp, prawn, pork fat, tiny pieces of fish.

Techniques: Float fishing, free-lining, spinning.

All three mullets are common in those waters where they can exist, which includes practically freshwater well upriver. The most common is the thick-lipped species and it is also the largest, reaching over 10lb (4.5kg).

Thick-lipped grey mullet
Chelon labrosus
Like all the mullets, this has a streamlined body with two dorsal fins, the first of which has four spines. It is dark green or grey above, with longitudinally-striped grey and silvery sides and a white belly. The upper lip is conspicuously broad.

Thin-lipped grey mullet
Liza ramada
This is very similar to the thick-lipped mullet, but with a narrow upper lip. It is smaller than *Chelon labrosus*, reaching about 6lb (2.7kg).

Golden grey mullet
Liza aurata
This fish is very like the thin-lipped species, but lacks the dark spot at the base of the pectoral fin. It has a golden spot on the gill cover.

The techniques and baits for taking mullet are the same for all three species. Locating a shoal is rarely a problem, as the fish are easily spotted with the aid of polarised sunglasses as they dimple the surface while feeding in the upper layers of the water. But catching them is quite a different matter. Beginners have said that they are uncatchable, but this is not the case, although they have highly developed senses and so the angler must use extreme caution. Mullet are rarely an easy target.

The tackle and methods are mainly those used in freshwater fishing. A rod suitable for tench or barbel is ideal, matched with a fixed-spool reel loaded with line of between 2 and 8lb (0.9-3.6kg) b.s. depending on conditions and the size of mullet anticipated.

Below: *Extremely timid, inshore mullet present a real challenge to the angler. There are three species; all are sleek, streamlined fish.*

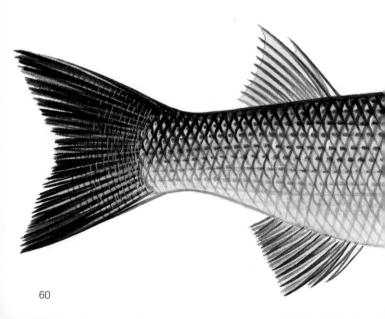

Use light tackle as far as possible, but it is unwise to drop to a very low b.s. in snaggy water or where there is the chance of a very big mullet. So far as hooks are concerned, a range from 8 to 16 is all that is needed.

When mullet are feeding close in, at or near the surface, a floating or slowly sinking bait presented on a free line is a simple but effective method.

A variation found to be successful for surface-feeding mullet out of normal casting range is to roll up a crust of bread and fix it by a couple of half-hitches of the line. The hook

Below: *With the rod tucked safely under his arm, this angler is seeking mullet that are feeding close to the wall of a stone breakwater.*

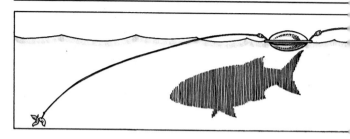

Above: *Mullet respond well to a slow-sinking bait fished on a bubble float rig. Part-filled with water, the float provides weight for casting but becomes extremely sensitive once in the water.*

Below: *A number of float patterns can be used for mullet, including a stick float fixed top and bottom, a waggler, and a slider with a depth stop (left). A Mepps Lure with a ragworm (right) is also effective.*

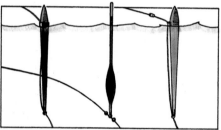

carries a tiny piece of flake, crust or paste. Dunk the roll to get it heavy with water, then cast out.

Once in the water the whole thing becomes a soggy mess, and mullet suck away at fragments breaking off. One fish will be sure to take the bait with the hook in it. The tell-tale sign will be when the line cuts away from the main bulk of the crust.

Float fishing is probably the best all-round method for taking mullet, using freshwater stick, waggler and slider-float patterns. Wherever a float is used it becomes possible to present a bait sensitively at whatever depth the mullet are feeding. It is particularly effective when worked down a tide or current. Plenty of groundbait and hookbait samples should be thrown in at frequent intervals.

The standard leger, and one or two-hook nylon paternoster rigs, are useful when mullet are feeding on the bottom or along a wall or rock face. It is important when legering to hold the rod at all times, feeling for bites by resting the fingers on the line, and striking as soon as a bite is felt.

Mullet are wary feeders and the bites they give can vary from quite strong pulls to gentle knocks and dips of the float or rod tip. Only experience can tell when to strike and when to wait for a more positive sign; what is vital is that the angler must keep alert at all times.

A hooked mullet of any size is a powerful fish and it is not wise to try to bully it over the rim of the landing net too quickly. Although the lips of these fish are leathery, the hook-hold is often very tenuous and any excessive pressure may tear the hook free.

Mullet must be played with patience, giving and recovering line smoothly, only applying pressure if the fish heads for a snag or thick weed. An ample landing net is essential.

Sometimes it is necessary to fish from a high point on rocks or a harbour wall, where a landing net is impossible to use. This is where the drop-net comes into its own, but the fish must be played out so that it lies quietly in the net. Never try to lift a big mullet up on the end of the line. It is sure to drop off.

Spinning is a killing method on some tidal estuaries. The standard Mepps or a traditional silver yellow-leaf bar-spoon, which is 1in (25mm) long and has a row of beads along the bar, are well-known successful lures. But whatever lure is selected, a small harbour ragworm must be draped round the treble hook.

In summer, spring tides heap masses of seaweed along the shore. This weed, rotting in the sun, is a breeding ground for many creatures and it is often full of maggots. By forking the weed into the sea round highwater mark it is possible to attract mullet to feed there, close to the edge, where they can find the maggots and other life that crawl from the weed.

Great fun can be had with a reservoir fly rod, size 8 or 9 line, a medium-strength leader and a polythene maggot-fly with one or two live bluebottles on the barb.

Casting the fly line enables the lure to be laid gently on the water without creating any commotion, presenting the bait in a very natural manner. Of all the ways to catch mullet, this is perhaps the most exciting approach.

Below: A light rod and fixed-spool reel brought this mullet in. Note the capacious and handy dropnet.

POLLACK and COALFISH

Waters: Wrecks, reefs, rocky headlands, rough ground, deepwater harbours.
Baits: Fish strips, squid, king ragworm, live prawn, sandeel, artificial lures.
Techniques: Float fishing, paternoster, drift fishing, trolling, jigging with feathers and artificial lures.

Both the pollack and the coalfish are widely distributed in northern European seas, the coalfish being more prolific in northern waters while the pollack is a favourite quarry of anglers who fish the many wrecks and reefs of the south-west, where it grows to its maximum size.

Pollack
Pollachius pollachius
Also known as the lythe, the pollack is a dark brown along the back, with a yellowish belly. There is no barbel, although the fish is closely related to the cod. A distinguishing feature is that the lower jaw projects beyond the upper; the eye is large in comparison with the head, and the lateral line arches over the pelvic fins. This fish can reach 25lb (11.3kg) in weight.

Coalfish
Pollachius virens
There is little to distinguish the coalfish from the pollack. Known also as the saithe, the coalfish's lower jaw does not protrude like that of the pollack, and there is usually a small barbel on the lower lip. The lateral line is not curved. Like the pollack, coalfish prefer deeper water and reach weights of over 25lb (11.3kg).

Fishing for both the coalfish and the pollack ranks among the best boat-fishing sport available to sea fishermen. Either species will give a splendid account of itself when hooked on sporting tackle which demands that the angler play the fish.

It is generally felt that reef fish fight harder than those hooked among deep wrecks, and there is reason to accept this supposition. If a pollack is brought up from the depths too quickly its swim-bladder will not have time to adjust. The result is that the fish is quickly in trouble and gives up before it gets halfway to the surface.

Whatever bait or lure is selected, its presentation is of paramount importance. It must be as lifelike as possible and with fish baits the long flowing trace is traditionally the best rig. Here, the most important item is the L-shaped boom made in stainless steel. The long arm should be at least 10in (25cm), to separate the trace from the main line as it sinks to the seabed.

The length of the trace is important when the fish are not biting freely. On slack tides the trace should be at its longest to give maximum effect as the retrieve begins, but these long traces can present problems because they tend to tangle. Great care must be taken when lowering the terminal tackle down to the seabed, but using a 15ft (4.5m) or even 20ft (6m) trace the angler will take fish to the frustration of less knowing anglers. In fast tides the trace can be shortened to 8-10ft (2.4-3m), the flow itself giving a vigorous movement to the bait.

Lower the tackle until it taps the bottom, then use a slow retrieve in a fast tide and a quick one in a slow tide; it is most important to keep the bait on the move at all times.

Rod selection is important too. It must be resilient enough to absorb the initial plunge of the fish, and some anglers think the ideal rod is a salmon-spinning rod coupled with a high-retrieve-ratio multiplier loaded with a few hundred yards (or metres) of 16 to 20lb (7-9kg) b.s. line.

Set the clutch so that a sudden dive will not break the line. It may feel as if the fish is going right back to the depths, but in fact they rarely go that far so slowly tighten the clutch and slow the fish down, then try retrieving line and fish.

Above: *A long flowing trace was used to reach this good pollack, caught from a drifting boat over rough ground off Ireland.*

Below: *In its element in the swirling water round reefs, the pollack is a worthy adversary for the angler who likes deepwater fishing.*

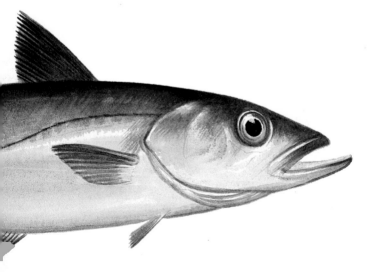

DOGFISH

Waters: Sandy areas (lesser spotted), rough and rocky ground (greater spotted), clean ground (spurdog), silty ground (smooth hound).
Baits: Fish such as mackerel, herring and pilchard; squid, hermit crab.
Techniques: General bottom fishing tactics with leger tackle.

All of these small sharks are widely distributed and fairly common all round the coast where they scavenge for animal food of all kinds. Both the spotted dogfishes and the spurdog are fished for commercially, being netted in great numbers and sold in fried fish shops as 'rock salmon'.

Spurdog
Squalus acanthias
This is a very common fish round the coasts of Europe, and sometimes congregates in huge shoals. Dark grey above, with a scattering of white spots, it is distinguished by the long, sharp spines in front of each of the two dorsal fins. It may grow to about 20lb (9kg).

Smooth hound
Mustelus mustelus; M. asterias
The smooth hounds are very similar in shape, size and habits, and are found over the same marks. Their coloration is a dull grey along the back with a creamy white underbelly. The visible difference between them is that *M. asterias*, also known as the starry smooth hound, has white spots on its back and sides. Both fish can grow to 30lb (13.6kg).

Greater spotted dogfish
Scyliorhinus stellaris
Also known as the bull huss or nursehound, this fish has a few large dark brown blotches on its greyish back, and a creamy white underside. It is a thick-bodied fish which grows to over 20lb (9kg), and it is found in small packs which move fast when hunting for food, mainly in deep water

Below: *A securely hooked spurdog about to come aboard. The nylon-covered wire trace provides a safety factor as the fish rolls.*

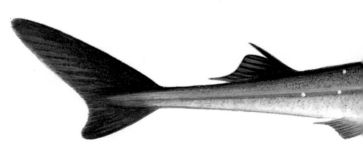

Above: *The only small shark with two spines, a spurdog must be handled with care. The species is suffering from over-fishing both by anglers and by commercial boats.*

Lesser spotted dogfish
Scyliorhinus canicula
The lesser spotted dogfish has numerous dark brown spots on a light, sandy brown back, shading to a whitish belly. A comparatively small fish, it rarely reaches 4lb (1.8kg).

Angling methods for all these fishes are similar. When fishing specifically

for spurdog, a light boat rod with a reel loaded with 15lb (6.8kg) b.s. nylon is adequate. The terminal tackle should consist of a single hook tied to a long trace of nylon stronger than the reel line.

Another favourite method is to use a paternoster rig with one or two snoods, the hooks baited with fish. A further hook can be added below the weight and tied to a long trace.

When hooked a large spurdog fights hard. Its sharp teeth, the mark of a predator, can quickly bite through a fine nylon line, so hooks tied to strong

Below: *The distinctive white spots show clearly on this smooth hound, which was taken on hermit crab fished from a boat.*

Above: *Competition anglers will often concentrate on the lesser spotted dogfish. Large packs often congregate on the bottom.*

nylon or even wire should be used. Nylon is preferred, however, for it is more pliable. If nylon is used it is advisable to use a net when lifting a big fish from the water.

The spines of the spurdog can inflict a nasty wound; they are not venomous, but the danger comes from harmful bacteria being introduced

Below: *The greater spotted dogfish, or nursehound or bull huss, can put up a dour struggle when hooked on sporting tackle.*

into a wound when a spine penetrates the skin. A traditional method of avoiding trouble is to cut the spines off with pliers before unhooking the fish. This is fine if the fish is to be kept, but if not it should be released unharmed.

The lesser spotted dogfish are the most common of this group and are encountered in the deeper marks as well as shallow bays. Some anglers regard them as a nuisance because they often take baits intended for other species, but during sea angling matches the dogfish has often been the means of amassing a winning weight.

The usual rig is a three-hook trace at least 8ft (2.4m) long, fitted below a free-running weight. This leger tackle is best when baited with fish strips and

small squid. When dogfish are located in a feeding mood sport can be hectic and a lot of fish may be boated.

Care should be taken when handling dogfish; when held by the head the fish may bend its body back around the hand, its very rough skin causing painful abrasions.

Smooth hounds are not easily located, but as with the dogfishes when they are found sport can be fast and furious. The best bait is hermit crab, used alive, on hook sizes either 1/0 or 2/0. If the hermit crabs are small two can be put on the same hook. The reason for this bait is that the diet of the smooth hound consists almost wholly of crabs and crustaceans.

Smooth hounds are smooth in name only, and the skin is in fact very rough. The nylon hook traces need to be of at least 25lb (11.3kg) b.s. to withstand the sandpapering action of this skin. Above the trace, the reel line b.s. can be as low as 15lb (6.8kg).

Smooth hounds are rugged fighters, fast and lively, and will certainly struggle furiously right to the boat. The smaller dogfish can be lifted from the water by hand, but all the larger ones need the assistance of a net.

Below: *Lifting a small dogfish in, caught on a strip of fresh mackerel. Unless it is wanted in competition, it should be released unharmed.*

TOPE *Galeorhinus galeus*

Waters: Inshore and offshore; estuaries, bays, tideraces over rough ground and gravel.
Baits: Mackerel, herring, small flatfish; whole, or in large fresh fillets.
Techniques: Running leger, general bottom fishing tactics, driftlining.

One of the smallest of the sharks, but also one of the most sporting, the tope is a fast and powerful swimmer with a streamlined body. It is fairly common in inshore waters where it hunts on the seabed. Coloration is a greyish-brown along the back and a lighter grey on the underside.

This sleek fish averages 30lb (13.6kg), but specimens are known of over 70lb (32kg). The nets of many commercial fishermen have been torn by this shark in its attempts to get at the food fish inside.

An advantage of tope fishing is that you do not need very expensive equipment. A 30lb (13.6kg) class rod, 6½-7ft (2m) long, with a multiplier or a centrepin capable of holding 200-300 yards or metres of 26-30lb (12-13.6kg) b.s. nylon is an ideal set-up.

The hook size must be judged according to the bait, and mounted on at least 15in (38cm) of nylon-covered

Below: The fish must be coaxed towards the boat – too much pressure and it will roll in the water, tangling and breaking the line.

Right: A tope caught on a running leger rig in the English Channel is drawn in close, ready to be tailed. Note the large-capacity reel.

wire of about 50-60lb (22.6-27kg)
b.s.; the tope's teeth will sever nylon.
Some tope anglers prefer a trace of
about 6ft (1.8m) so that the rough
body of the tope does not cut through
the line. This usually happens because
too much pressure is put on the fish
when it is being played. Unable to

head in the direction it chooses, the
tope merely spins in the water,
wrapping the line round its body.

Below: *The tope is a slender-bodied
shark with a large upper lobe to the
tail, and a rough skin which can cut
nylon line.*

Above: *Taken from a shallow sandy bay on the west coast of Ireland, this 35lb (16kg) tope was tailed by the boatman and returned.*

Attach the weight to a Clement's boom so that the length of the trace can be varied as the tide changes. During fast tides as much as 30ft (9m) of line can be pulled through the boom before putting on a matchstick stop. This can be snapped off quickly by a companion when a hooked tope is drawn alongside, allowing the lead and boom to slide down to the swivel.

A variety of baits can be used, bearing in mind that they must be fresh. Favourites are mackerel, whiting, dabs and, in estuaries, silver-eel tails. A large mackerel will make two tope baits. Small whiting make an ideal bait used whole. Garfish too make good bait, and large ones can be cut into two or three chunks.

Dabs of 8-9in (20-23cm) can be fished flat, or the fish can be cut on the white side from head to tail just through to the backbone. Bringing the two sides together, white side out, makes a flatfish into a roundfish, which can be a more effective bait.

All the round fish should have the line threaded through with a baiting-needle, so that the hook can be attached near the head while the wire snood comes out through the tail. For large baitfish, hooks of size 8/0 to 10/0 are advised, size 6/0 being sufficient for smaller baits.

When tope fishing the first take often comes very quickly after the bait has reached the seabed. The first indication when fishing from an anchored boat is a nice, bouncy bite, quickly followed by line being taken off the spool – slowly at first but building up to a full-blooded run. This can vary, sometimes as much as 150 yards (137m), or as little as 30 yards (27m).

Do not strike until the tope has made its first run; it will pause for a second or two, then move off again on a slightly slower run. This is the time to strike – and it must be a very powerful strike in order to take up the slack which will have built up in the line.

Once hooked, the tope's reactions are different every time. One common habit is to head straight back towards the boat, and the problem is to recover line as fast as possible to regain contact with the fish. As the tope tires, work it towards the boat, but do not exert too much pressure or it will swim in a spiral and roll itself up in the line.

Tope should not be killed, and it is not necessary to use a gaff, so when the fish is alongside and played out get the skipper to grab the tailfin in one hand and a pectoral fin in the other and lift in inboard. Remove the hook and put the fish back.

When the first tope has been caught, waste no time in getting the bait down again. Tope of 20-30lb (9-13.6kg) tend to shoal, so several fish can be caught in quick succession. Only the very large tope, 40lb (18kg) and over adopt a solitary existence.

Below: *A second pair of hands is essential to hold the tope steady, while the angler carefully removes the hook using pliers.*

CONGER *Conger conger*

Waters: Offshore wrecks, reefs, rocky ground, harbours.
Baits: Oily fish, pilchard, squid.
Techniques: Running leger, fixed leger.

The conger grows to immense sizes, and even the rod-caught record is over 100lb (45kg). Deepwater wrecks hold the largest specimens, but harbour piles and inshore rock formations can provide homes for very sizeable ones. The fish has a dark back and a grey-white belly, and is quite scaleless.

When young, conger feed out among the kelp in inshore areas, then move out to sea for larger food. They scavenge for dead and dying fish and other sea animals before eventually settling in a permanent lair.

Once in its lair a conger is extremely difficult to dislodge. If a hooked fish is given the chance to get even half of its long muscular body back into its home it will become immoveable. It wedges itself into the wreck or between the rocks and refuses to budge, no matter how much pressure the angler exerts.

Only the best rod and reel will stand up to regular congering. A 30lb (13.6kg) class rod is usual, and some specialists prefer the security of a 50lb (22.6kg) rod. A 4/0 multiplier with an efficient clutch is the smallest reel that is suitable, and it should be loaded with 30-40lb (13.6-18kg) b.s. nylon. With a 50lb rod and a 6/0 reel, the line should be of 50lb b.s.

Braided lines are unsuitable for deepwater fishing, the reason being that their greater diameter compared to single-strand nylon produces more resistance to the tidal flow, causing the line to bow to an unacceptable degree.

The terminal rig is wire or heavy-duty nylon for the trace, about 18in (45cm) long and with a b.s. of not less than 150lb (68kg). This is connected by crimps to a 10/0 hook with an offset point, and a 5/0 swivel. Fished as a sliding leger, the weight can be attached to a small plastic carrier or by light nylon to a swivel.

This is a weak link, and it is deliberate. It acts as a 'rotten bottom' so if the tackle becomes lodged in an obstruction a good tug usually breaks the light nylon and all that is left on the sea bed is the weight. The range of weights carried should be between 8oz (226kg) and 2lb (900g).

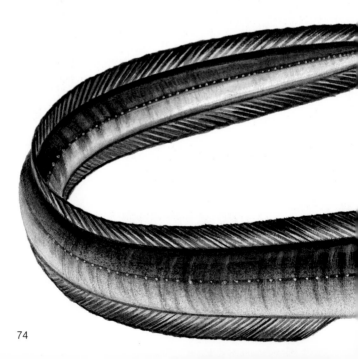

Above: *Robin Potter with the massive record-breaking conger of 109lb 6oz (66.4kg), caught in 1976 near the Eddystone lighthouse.*

Below: *All teeth and muscle, the conger is the toughest adversary any angler is likely to have to manhandle from the depths.*

Fresh mackerel and squid are the principal baits. The mackerel can be fished whole or in pieces; two fillets attached to the head, or tail, work well. A squid head with its tentacles is a superb conger bait, while the body can be cut into 4in (10cm) wide strips, each cut into points.

The technique of wrecking for conger is quite different to reef fishing. The fish often react to a bait more decisively than when on rocky ground, so the rod should be held all the time the bait is on the bottom. Bite detection provides no problem. The rod tip pulls down hard, followed by strong 'knocks'. You must give a few feet of line immediately, to take the pressure off the terminal tackle. Wait a while, then recover surplus line until the bulk of the conger is felt. When it feels this pull it will back away, shaking its head.

This will tell all you need to know, and you must strike the hook home with two or three solid sweeps of the rod. Then start to pump the fish off the bottom as soon as possible. Speed here is vital, because the conger must be drawn into clear water before it can find somewhere to wedge itself in.

When playing a conger set the reel clutch to give line under maximum pressure; this gradually weakens the fish, and patience and a smooth pumping action will get the conger within gaffing range.

When that moment comes, snap the reel out of gear and stand clear. Often, the moment the conger feels the gaff it makes a violent lunge for freedom and if the reel is free there is no chance of line breakage.

Right: *An average conger, but it put up a good struggle when hooked in the depths of a rocky mark off Stromness, Orkneys.*

Below: *This giant centrepin reel was specially made for bringing up fish such as conger from deepwater marks. The large diameter increases the retrieve rate.*

LING *Molva molva*

Waters: Reefs, wrecks, rocky ground.
Baits: Whole mackerel, other fish baits, squid, artificial lures.
Techniques: Leger, general bottom-fishing, paternoster, drift-fishing, baited feathers, jigging.

A member of the cod family, the ling is a long fish, reaching over 6ft (1.8m) in length and over 50lb (22kg) in weight. A predator, it is a powerful swimmer and must be drawn into open water immediately after being hooked. It is a voracious feeder in and around the wrecks and rocks of the seabed where it lives. Adult ling, those over 15lb (6.8kg), keep beyond the 10-fathom (18m) mark and the greatest catches are taken from deep-water wrecks. Tremendous sport can be had throughout the year, the peak season being between November and March when the ling congregate prior to spawning. Huge numbers of ling of between 10lb and 50lb (4.5-22.6kg) often inhabit wrecks, and rough ground also attracts the fish which keep to the lower levels of reefs. Here, 30lb (13.6kg) ling are often found.

Tackle must be strong, for a ling hooked in over 40 fathoms (73m) can put up a powerful struggle. Most wreck anglers use a 30lb (13.6kg) class rod, with a 4/0 or 6/0 multiplier loaded with line of at least 30lb b.s. With multiple-hook terminal rigs, the rod should be in the 50lb (22.6kg) class.

The rig should be a straight paternoster with two or three double snoods in about 80lb (36kg) b.s. nylon. Hook size is 8/0, preferably the Shaugnessy pattern, used with the conventional leger rig.

A 3/0 swivel connects the 2ft (60cm) trace to the reel line; above this swivel the weight is attached by light monofilament. If the lead fouls the wreckage a steady pull will snap this and nothing but the weight is lost. This is called a 'rotten bottom' and it is always sensible to incorporate it in a sea fishing terminal trace.

When using whole mackerel bait, delay the strike to give the ling time to swallow, because this fish does not bite cleanly, but just tears and gulps its prey. Another fine ling bait is a squid head, its waving tentacles being highly rated as an attractor.

During the first few minutes after a big ling has been hooked no quarter must be given and the clutch on the multiplier should be set to prevent the fish from taking more than a few feet of line. Once the fish is in clear water, ease the clutch to suit the strength of the line. The struggle will not last too long because ling are affected by a rapid change in water pressure, and from 30 fathoms (55m) the fight is over by the time they are halfway to the surface, all strong resistance having ended.

If the fish is brought up slowly, it has time to adjust its swimbladder to the change in pressure and gives a much livelier fight.

Wreck ling can be caught while fishing on the drift or from an anchored boat. But the risk of snagging a hook or weight fast in a wreck is high when drifting, so the 'rotten bottom' attachment is invaluable. Most of the big winter hauls of ling are made as the boat slowly drifts over a wreck, but success depends on wind direction related to

the position of the wreck and the strength of the tide. An experienced skipper will allow for these factors to give the angler the best chance.

Drifting also allows the use of pirks, which can be used bare or baited. Artificial eels are another fine ling attractor and should be attached by two short snoods on a tough nylon paternoster. Some anglers prefer to use nylon-covered wire.

Pirking and paternostering with artificials is tiring because it is essential to keep the terminal rig constantly on the move. But this activity can be a boon if the weather is cold, because sitting still in a boat soon results in cold hands and feet.

Fishing for ling over rough ground – a mixture of sand and mud, boulders and grit – can be exciting, but in these areas ling rarely weigh more than 30lb (13.6kg), the really big ones preferring the dark confines of wrecks. Rough-ground ling average about 15lb (6.8kg), but there is a consolation in that fish of this size make very good eating.

For reef ling, a 20lb (9kg)-class rod and 4/0 multiplier loaded with 20-25lb (9-11.3kg) b.s. nylon is more than adequate. The terminal trace should be a short leger with a 6/0 hook. Pirks and other artificials seldom bring good results when fished over reefs, but they work well over wrecks.

Below: *While related to the cod, the ling lives like the conger, hunting live food in the black depths of reefs and wrecks.*

Above: *This ling has gorged the bait. It was hooked from a reef mark off the Cornish coast. The bait was squid fished on a trace.*

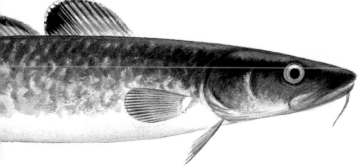

RAYS

Waters: Sandy bays (undulate), offshore sandbanks (blonde, small-eyed), shallows over sand, shingle and mud (thornback), estuaries and silty shallows (stingray), deepwater marks (cuckoo and starry rays).
Baits: Most fishbaits, crustaceans, squid, cuttlefish strip, marine worms, live sandeel.
Techniques: Free-running leger, paternoster-leger.

The group of fishes called the rays are not flatfishes, such as the turbot, plaice and so on. Rays belong to the cartilaginous fishes, those with soft bones. They are very widely distributed, being caught from all kinds of fishing grounds in European seas.

Thornback ray
Raja clavata
Numerous spines along the back and tail distinguish the thornback from other rays. This fish is also known as the roker, and is the most abundant ray. Coloration varies, in general being a mottled brown, with black and cream spots. It is a shallow-water fish reaching over 30lb (13.6kg).

Right: *The thornback, just one of the ray group. It is easily recognised by the spines along the dorsal area. This one is a male.*

Below: *A basic running leger rig with a long trace is ideal for ray fishing. The weight is clipped to a Clement's boom.*

Blonde ray
Raja brachyura
The blonde ray is the largest of the rays, going to nearly 40lb (18kg). It is a light brown colour with many small dark spots extending to the margins of the upper surface.

Above: *A thornback being played to the surface. It was hooked on tackle fished well down-tide.*

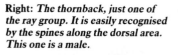

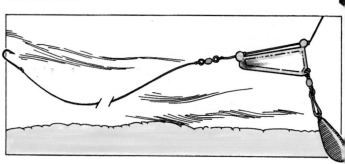

Undulate ray
Raja undulata
The colour pattern of the undulate ray varies from dark to a light brown, with an irregular pattern of dark stripes edged with white spots. A southerly fish, it reaches about 20lb (9kg).

Sting ray
Dasyatis pastinaca
The stingray is named for the venomous barb at the end of the tail. It is a dangerous weapon and can be used to considerable effect when the fish is handled wrongly. This ray can reach 60lb (27kg) or more.

Small-eyed ray
Raja microocellata
The size of its eyes gives the small-eyed ray its name, smaller than those of the other rays. It is a southern species and is also known as the painted ray. The greyish-brown upperside has irregular white lines. It reaches about 16lb (7.2kg).

Cuckoo ray
Raja naevus
The cuckoo ray is one of the smallest rays, one of 5lb (2.2kg) being considered a specimen. The wings are rounded and carry a dark circular spot

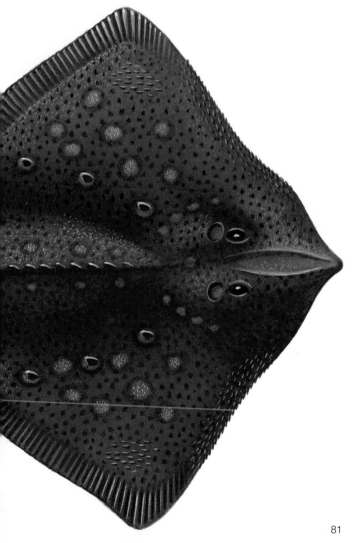

with yellow dots on each side. The upper surface is light brown and is covered by small spines. It is a deepwater fish.

Rays are quite common in many areas during the summer months, many of them moving into inshore waters in the spring. At the approach of winter they head for deepwater again. Sizeable thornbacks in particular are taken off piers and beaches.

Tackle need not be powerful, a rod in the 30lb (13.6kg) class being adequate so long as it has plenty of action. Where tides are easy and in quiet bays the tackle can be scaled down to a 20lb (9kg) outfit. Multiplier reels are generally used, loaded with line of about 25-30lb (11.3-13.6kg) b.s. depending on local conditions and tide strengths. Light tackle enthusiasts now go down to line as fine as 12-15lb (5.4-6.8kg) b.s. if conditions allow.

Rays are bottom-living fish, so that is where the bait must be presented. Legering is the obvious method. A simple running leger with one or two hooks on a strong flowing trace rig at least 4ft (1.2m) long is ideal; the trace length should be increased if the tide is quickening. The lightest weight that will hold bottom should be used, attached by a Clement's boom.

When a ray is boated and the hook removed, the nylon trace should always be checked carefully since the grinding teeth of these fish will chafe line badly.

Rays are not finicky feeders but the best bait is a thick slice from a fillet of freshly caught mackerel, or the tail section cut diagonally. Slices of other fish can be used too, as well as crab and squid. Often, a whole small fish such as a sprat or a live sandeel will attract rays, especially the blonde rays in the vicinity of sandbanks.

After dark is the best time for the beachcaster, when rays move in closer to the shore. At such times the fish feed on small crabs, so that is the recommended bait.

Stingrays are not uncommon, so every ray should be checked before it is handled. If the sharp, poisonous spine is seen (and sometimes this is

Above: *Fresh from the sea, a 24lb (11kg) blonde ray caught in a strong tide race off the Scilly Isles. The bait was legered fish.*

Above: *Mackerel, the first-choice sea angling bait. Its silvery, flashing skin and oily flesh are the two prime attractors for other fish.*

difficult when the fish is thrashing about on the surface) let the skipper or an experienced angler deal with it. The serrated spine can inflict a painful and dangerous wound. Even the thornback ray should be handled with care, for although the spines are not venomous, they will be dirty and if they penetrate the skin harmful bacteria can be introduced into the wound, leading to a painful infection. The jaws of rays are also to be kept away from. They do not have pointed teeth, but crushing teeth, and if a finger is gound between them the angler's fishing may for a while be severely curtailed.

Above: *This undulate ray is being tagged and returned unharmed to the water. It was caught from a shallow sandy bay on a squid bait.*

Below: *A thornback lying on a bed of gravel. Note how the unevenly patterned back of the fish blends*

Above: *A stingray caught from a deep, sandy mark off the Irish coast. Bait was the ever-popular mackerel – a large fresh slice.*

into the background. Also known as the roker, this ray can be caught on a wide variety of baits.

SKATE

Waters: Sandy and muddy seabeds, occasionally rough ground, all depths.
Baits: Fish, live or dead: mackerel, herring, dab, small flatfish, large fillets of fresh fish.
Techniques: Legering, other bottom-fishing methods from shore and boat.

There are three species of these huge fish in European waters and apart from biological differences they can be treated the same so far as fishing is concerned.

Common skate
Raja batis
The common skate is just that. It reaches 400lb (180kg) although those taken on rod and line are more likely to be between 100 and 200lb (45-90kg). The back is a slate-grey, with dark and light coloured spots. This skate has decreased in numbers in the past decade owing to commercial netting, but angling too has taken its toll. In some areas the species is protected, so that all fish taken by anglers must be returned to the water alive.

White skate
Raja alba
The white skate has a pointed nose and a more triangular body shape. Also known as the bottle-nosed skate, it is a brownish-grey on the upper side, with white underneath. There are numbers of prickles on both sides. A white skate of 100lb (45kg) is a fine angling catch, but commercial fishermen have been known to net fish weighing over 500lb (227kg).

Below: *Playing a small skate to the boat. The tackle, not too heavy, is a boat rod and a multiplier reel; bait was a slice of mackerel.*

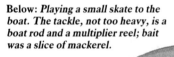

Long-nosed skate
Raja oxyrinchus
Well described by its name, this is a deepwater species. It is darkish brown on the back and greyish below, and while anglers have taken specimens over 100lb (45kg), fish of three times that weight have been netted.

The three species of skate caught by anglers are all very large fish, and some degree of expertise is needed to make a certain identification when one is boated. All can easily reach high weights, so size is no guide to whether a fish is a common, long-nosed or white skate.

Above: *The common skate, also called the blue or grey skate, is possibly the most prolific of the skates found in deep waters of 300 fathoms (140m) or so, but anglers cannot reach these depths.*

Most skate fishing is done from anchored boats in deep water. Big skate do move into shallow, sandy bays and there are known marks where this happens, although some have sadly been so over-fished that the skate are no longer in evidence. Where skate still occur in the shallows the tackle can be scaled down to suit the conditions.

Shore anglers rarely fish specifically for big skate, but the occasional one is taken, usually when the angler casts from a harbour wall for other species.

These large, bulky fish require the use of powerful tackle, such as a rod in the 30-50lb (13.6-22.6kg) class with a length of 6-8ft (1.8-2.4m). This should be fitted with a large multiplier reel, such as a 4/0 or 6/0, loaded with line of at least 30lb (13.6kg) b.s.

The single hook, size 6/0 to 8/0, should be attached to 12-18in (30-46cm) of strong wire, connected by a heavy-duty swivel to a wire trace at

Above: A choppy swell makes life uncomfortable for these anglers, fishing a deepwater mark for big skate. The area, off the Orkneys, also holds huge halibut.

least 5ft (1.5m) long and of about 50lb (22.6kg) b.s.

Of all the fish species that can be used as bait in skate fishing, one that is rarely considered is the dogfish. It is thought that small dogfish, which spend a lot of time on the seabed, form a large proportion of a skate's diet, but the angler will need a great deal of nerve to spend a few hours of his angling time with a live dogfish as bait!

The prime choice is fresh mackerel, invariably fished right down on the bottom, so the weight of lead will be decided by the strength of the tide and the depth of water beneath the boat.

When the deep marks are being fished, ones known to hold large skate, the bait should be left for some

Above: *The author with a common skate of about 80lb (36kg), caught from a deepwater mark at the outer edge of a sandy bay. It took a deep-fished mackerel bait.*

time without being disturbed. The line should however be watched or felt regularly, for crabs can quickly rip any fishbait to pieces. Their unwelcome attentions will be felt as vibrations on the line.

In order to take a bait, a skate must first settle over it, owing to the ventral position of the mouth. When it does this one of its wings will touch the line and this movement can be mistaken for a bite. Any strike at this stage may well result in the wing of the fish being foul-hooked, or the skate may be scared off and lost.

So, after the first indication of the skate's wing brushing the bait, the bite will follow, registered by a definite motion of the top of the rod,

steadily bending down – and because of the weight and strength of the skate the rod top will keep on bending.

Remembering that even a medium-sized skate is in the order of 100lb (45kg), and that its flattened shape allows it to hug the seabed very closely, the angler will find that the fish is practically immovable. Hauling on the rod will achieve nothing but a bend in the rod – assuming the line doesn't break. But a continual, severe pressure will eventually lift the skate, or persuade it to move off the bottom. More muscle-straining effort will raise its nose and then, and only then, the real struggle begins.

Reeling a big skate up from deep water is a matter of stamina; it has been described as like trying to pull a grand piano up the side of a lighthouse. Once a large skate has been hooked, fought and finally boated, the angler will sleep well that night – the sleep of exhaustion.

SMALL FLATFISH

Waters: Shallow sandy bays (dab), offshore sandbanks and sandy bays (plaice), harbours and estuaries (flounders).
Baits: Hermit crab, soft crab, shrimp, cockle, lugworm, ragworm, sandeel, squid and cuttlefish strips.
Techniques: Float, baited spoon, leger.

Flatfishes are remarkable in that having started life as normal, round fishes, they soon develop a 'wandering eye' which travels right round the fish's head towards the other eye. The fish spends the rest of its life on one side, its mouth being distorted to suit.

Plaice
Pleuronectes platessa
The plaice can be recognised by the bright orange spots on the brownish background of its upperside. It is quite common, being found mainly in deepish water. Specimens of over 6lb (2.7kg) have been taken on rod and line, but 10lb (4.5kg) plaice have been netted commercially.

Flounder
Platicthys flesus
Similar to the plaice in appearance, the flounder is dull brown or greenish brown, with a line of small prickles along the base of the dorsal fin and anal fin. It is unusual in being able to live in fresh water, and it is often taken by anglers well upriver. It may grow to about 6lb (2.7kg).

Sole
Solea solea
The soles are oval in shape, with the mouth right at the tip of the head. Coloration varies, but is generally dark brown with a few much darker blotches. This fish feeds mainly at night, and on occasion specimens of about 5lb (2.2kg) are taken.

Dab

Limanda limanda

Smallest of the flatfish, the dab can be identified by the rough feel when rubbed from tailfin to head. It has a light brown upperside, with a few dark yellowish spots. The average weight is about 8oz (226g), but dabs of just over 2lb (900g) are known.

Although flatfish do not care for rocky ground, they are to be found in the patches of sand often distributed among rocks. In particular, they favour sandy areas round reefs of offshore wrecks.

A good flatfish mark is where the bottom is mud and sand or a mixture

Below: *The plaice is unmistakable; the nodules running from between the eyes are a main feature. Plaice can hybridise with flounders.*

Above: *The head of a flounder, a typical bottom-living flatfish, showing how both eyes are placed on one side of the head.*

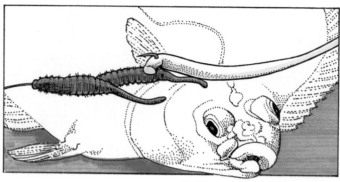

Above: *A cocktail bait of lug and squid tentacle undulates past the hungry eyes of a flattie.* **Good bait presentation is essential for angling success, with all fish.**

Right: *A 3½lb (1.6kg) plaice which fell to a long strip of squid fished on light tackle.* **The boat was over an offshore sandbank.**

of both. At all times of the year flatfish can be taken from inshore marks, and long casting is not necessary. The inshore habits of flatties also mean that piers and breakwaters are good places for seeking them.

Rod selection depends on the areas to be fished. From dinghies and in most harbours and sheltered estuaries, a light freshwater rod is adequate. On those estuaries where there is a fierce tiderun, the tackle needs to be stepped up to cope with this. When fishing from an open shore, or perhaps from rocks, piers or jetties, a light beachcasting rod may be more appropriate.

When fishing leger tackle for flounders, it is best to hold the rod at all times and feel for bites. This gives a more direct contact with the bait and what is happening to it. It is also advisable to keep the bait moving. If bites are not forthcoming, a few turns of the reel handle will lift and move the weight. This disturbs the silt, which in turn can attract the attentions of any flounder, or other flattie, that may be lying nearby.

Although flounders are bottom feeders they will rise off the seabed to take a tasty morsel which is fished in midwater. This is why on occasion some fine specimens are caught when the angler is float fishing. Here the baited spoon comes into its own.

Flounder spoons come in various sizes; they are light and generally of white plastic. The spoon blade revolves but not the trailing hook, which is baited with lug or ragworm.

This tackle is most effective when trotted down with the tide. The baited spoon can also be fished on a paternoster. The style can be practised from a boat, pier or any projecting structure.

Offshore sandbanks, especially those where sandeels are found, make fine plaice marks. The best tactic is to fish from a boat when the tide is running, during their feeding period.

Boat fishing for plaice needs a light 12lb (5.4kg) class rod, with matching line, and a heavy lead. One or two 1/0 longshank hooks, each baited with a cocktail of lugworm and long, thin strips of squid, complete the rig.

When drifting over sandbanks a running leger is the best tackle, using a Kilmore boom or leger link to attach a light weight and a flowing trace of about 20ft (6m).

Above: *Beachfishing took these two flatfish. The larger one is a flounder, and the smaller is a dab. The outfit was a light rod mounted with a small multiplier.*

Below: *A specimen sole of 5lb (2.2kg) taken during a night fishing session, long-casting off a beach. The fish put up a good struggle on lugworm and squid cocktail bait.*

LARGE FLATFISH

Waters: Shallow areas over shell, grit and sandbanks; fairly deep water over sand, sometimes near wrecks or reefs (turbot, brill), deep offshore waters (halibut).

Baits: Live sandeel, sprats, cuttlefish, squid; long, thin strips of fish; mackerel, small fish and crabs.

Techniques: Leger, paternoster, drift fishing.

This group includes some of the biggest flatfish, including the largest of them all, the mighty halibut, capable of reaching 500lb (227kg). Like their smaller relatives, the larger flatties begin life as tiny round fishes, and undergo a metamorphosis as they mature, becoming transformed into broad, flattened fish well adapted to living on the sea bed.

Below: *Scaleless, with bony nodules on the body, the turbot is keenly sought by anglers fishing the large sandbanks where it lives and feeds.*

92

Halibut
Hippoglossus hippoglossus
This is a deepwater fish found mainly in northern waters. It is brownish on the upperside and white beneath. It prefers strong tides over a sand or gravel bottom and feeds in midwater, hunting fish voraciously. It may grow to over 8ft (2.4m) long, but such fish are rare.

Turbot
Scophthalmus maximus
The diamond-shaped turbot is light brown on top, with numerous spots and a few tubercles. The spots extend to the tip of the tail. This fish is widely distributed, being found over sandy or gravelly bottoms. Well known for its eating qualities, it grows to at least 50lb (22.6kg).

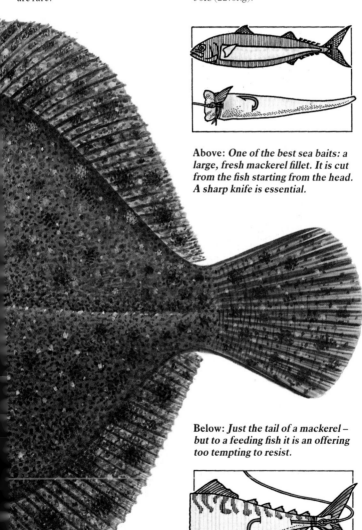

Above: *One of the best sea baits: a large, fresh mackerel fillet. It is cut from the fish starting from the head. A sharp knife is essential.*

Below: *Just the tail of a mackerel – but to a feeding fish it is an offering too tempting to resist.*

Brill

Scophthalmus rhombus

Although similar to the turbot, the brill only reaches some 16lb (7.2kg). It is brownish, with light and dark speckles. There are no tubercles on the top, and the fish is more rounded than its larger relative. It is found in sandy inshore areas, again preferring places where there is a strong tide flow. Being uncommon, not many are hooked on rod and line.

Fishing for large flatfish requires a thorough understanding of their feeding habits.

Headlands where fast currents pass over sandbanks provide rich feeding for turbot, which seek small fish caught up in the turbulent water. Such currents also produce banks of shell grit or soft sand in the bays beyond the race, and this is the type of seabed that carries the turbot's most important item of diet – the sandeel.

The season when sandeels are most abundant is between May and October, so the best time for turbot lies between those months. However, these fish are also taken during January and early February, probably having been drawn inshore by the movement of the sprat shoals.

The best way to contact turbot is to fish during small to medium tides, and when light winds allow for drift fishing. Long traces of anything up to 25ft (7.6m) will allow baits to be worked just off the seabed with the minimum amount of lead. Live

Above: *Hooked on a bait of live sandeel, a turbot hugs the seabed and puts a good bend in the rod.*

sandeels or fresh dead ones are the best baits. The alternative is thin, white strips of mackerel, garfish or squid. But when drift fishing these must be cut to resemble sandeel.

When strong tides and adverse winds prohibit drift fishing, you can either bounce the same bait along the bottom or secure it while at anchor. However, experience shows that the turbot are less willing to pursue baits at these times.

When turbot are about, baits are seldom rejected, so take your time in striking. In fact, because the mouth is of bone and thin membrane it is best to ease the hook home instead of giving a powerful heave. Steady pressure is all that is needed to bring the fish to the surface. There will be occasional 'bumps' but rarely a struggle.

Bait presentation is all-important when fishing for these predators, and long traces are essential. The use of a boom standing away from the reel line eliminates the chance of the trace becoming entangled when fishing slow tides.

Brill have roughly the same lifestyle as the turbot. But fewer are taken than turbot, perhaps because of their smaller reproductive capacity. When taken they are usually found over the same grounds and fished with the same bait and tackle as for turbot. Brill to about 3lb (1.3kg) are found inshore, over coarse sand or grit, feeding on small sandeels and fish fry.

For halibut, drift fishing is essential, with rods in the 30-50lb (13.6-22.6kg) class, and a 4/0 or 6/0 multiplier, loaded with 30-50lb b.s. line. A long trace of wire is recommended of about 25lb (11.3kg)

Below: *These two brill were hooked off the coast of Alderney. This fish and the turbot can hybridise, and some of the offspring are fertile.*

b.s., with a 6/0 hook. Weight depends on the tide. Any of the large fish baits can be used, or squid.

Halibut can be caught by trolling, or on a baited pirk, but whatever method is used, when a halibut is hooked and played to the boat the angler must be always on the alert, for these huge and powerful fish can suddenly make an unstoppable plunge back to the depths, and the unwary angler will find either the rod or the line broken in a flash.

SHARKS

Waters: Offshore marks (blue), inshore (thresher), reefs, rocky headlands, cliffs (porbeagle, occasionally thresher).
Baits: Live or dead fish such as mackerel, herring, pouting, small pollack, sprat, sandeel.
Techniques: Drift fishing, float fishing, trolling, free-lining.

Three shark species, the porbeagle, thresher and blue, are the main quarry for anglers, while the occasional mako and hammerhead provide an exciting tussle when they are hooked. Even the great white shark of Zane Grey fame has been reported off Britain.

Porbeagle
Lamna nasus
The porbeagle is fairly widely distributed, but found mostly off the Cornish coast where it often comes within a mile of the shore. It can be recognised by its portly shape and the keel-like ridges situated along each side of the tail. One of the larger species, it reaches over 500lb (226kg).

Thresher
Alopias vulpinus
This is the most easily recognised species of shark, because of its characteristic extended and curved upper tailfin lobe. Also known as the mackerel shark, it has been known to follow mackerel shoals close inshore. It can weigh well over 300lb (136kg).

Blue shark
Prionace glauca
The bluish-coloured back of the blue shark is very distinctive, and another characteristic is the rather long, pointed snout. This semi-tropical shark enters British waters as the seas warm up with the summer sun. This fish is a prime target for the growing number of sharking boats, but although it can reach at least 200lb (90kg), 60lb (27kg) is the average.

Fishing for shark needs very little in the way of tackle variations, for the technique is the same for all species. The only difference is in the strength of gear needed and the area selected. Basically the method is drifting, using

Above: *Bulky and powerful, the porbeagle is sought by anglers because of its power when hooked. Small ones sometimes come close inshore, but are not dangerous.*

Right: *The typical shark lower jaw: the teeth are replaced when lost and each species has a distinctive form of tooth serration. Study on living sharks is not recommended.*

Above: *The distinctive whip-like tail of the thresher makes it easily recognisable. This 200lb (90kg) fish was taken off the Isle of Wight.*

a large float to support a whole fish bait. This, dead or alive, can be presented at all levels from the seabed to just below the surface in a rubby-dubby trail.

The porbeagle offers the best opportunity for anglers to enjoy big-game fishing in European waters. This large shark comes in close under headlands and cliffs and even shallow water. It is a powerful fish demanding a rod about 7ft (2m) long in the 50-80lb (22.6-36kg) class, with a large-capacity reel to match, such as a Penn 6/0 or 9/0, with several hundred yards of at least 50lb (22.6kg) b.s. line.

A large hook, 10/0 or 12/0, is attached to a 2-3ft (60-90cm) wire trace, connected by a quick-release swivel to a further 12-15ft (3.6-4.5m) of wire trace complete with heavy duty connecting swivels. Nylon-covered wire is not recommended, and many keen sharkers prefer yacht-rigging wire. All the line attachments are made using crimps.

Up to three mackerel can be used on one hook, the barb going through

three pairs of eyes. Single baitfish are threaded on to the line with the hook protruding through the side or belly. The float can be anything buoyant – a balloon, large cork, or a lump of polystyrene.

The tackle can be reduced in strength for blues, a 50lb (22.6kg) outfit being adequate, and the boat needs to go out at least ten miles before starting the drift.

When feeding, shark will take squid, cuttlefish, or crab, but their main food supply is fish in the form of mackerel, herring, pouting, whiting, small pollack and pilchard, so any of these can be used as bait.

One item that is common to all shark fishing is the use of rubby-dubby. This consists of fish pieces and guts, preferably from oily fish, chopped and minced with bran, with a liberal quantity of fish oil. And to make the mixture truly attractive – to sharks – add some blood if it can be obtained from a local slaughterhouse. All this is well mashed and mixed, then tipped or poured into a sack which is stored in a bin until the mark is reached.

At the mark, hang the sack over the side of the boat so that it does not become fully covered. The roll of the boat, plus a tug now and again on the rope, will release the mixture, including tiny pieces of fish, to create a slick running away from the boat.

Roving shark find this slick irresistible and will head towards the source as if following a radar beam. Their feeding instincts roused, any bait fish suspended in the slick is likely to be snapped up. The scent travels a long way and in time shark will be attracted from some miles away.

If they do not take a bait, shark will literally come right up to the boat, so always have a number of baits out when the rubby-dubby is at work.

The usual indication that a shark has taken is that the float bobs about – consider it a warning – then float and line will begin to take off with a long run, pulling line off the reel. Do not strike at this stage; the run will stop and the float may even appear on the surface. Then another run will start, fast this time, and this is the moment

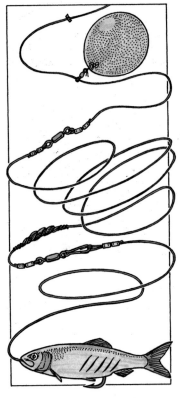

Above: *A shark rig. From the top: a line stop, float, crimped heavy-duty swivel, Jardine lead, and quick-release heavy-duty swivel. A baiting needle is used to thread the line through the bait, and the hook is attached afterwards.*

Below: *The float for a shark-fishing rig may be quite crude – any buoyant object will do, such as a lump of expanded polystyrene attached to the reel line using a simple clove hitch.*

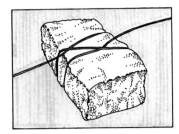

**Above: *Spray flies in all directions
as a porbeagle feels the gaff and
vainly tries to break free. This is not
the moment for angling novices to
become closely involved.***

to strike – hard, and again very hard.
This should ensure the shark is well
hooked and fighting mad. Another
run will occur, up to a hundred yards
of line hissing off the reel.

When that first run starts, all the
other anglers must retrieve their
tackle as fast as possible. There are
two reasons for this: a hooked shark
might run all the way round the boat,
creating an awful tangle of lines and

gear, and secondly another shark
might be hooked. It is not wise to try
to play two sharks at the same time for
fear of losing both through tangles.

The fish should be thoroughly
played out before any attempt is made
to land it. A lively shark is not only a
danger to the angler – it will cause
havoc on the boat by thrashing about
among the tackle and equipment.
Naturally a gaff is essential when
sharking, and two gaffs may be
needed to make quite sure of the fish.
Sharks, even small ones, are very
powerful creatures, and should be
handled with respect. They are not a
quarry for the inexperienced angler.

MONKFISH *Squatina squatina*

Waters: Inshore, where there are sandy and silty bays; occasionally on rough ground.
Baits: General fishbaits, mackerel, herring, pouting, small flatfish.
Techniques: Running leger from boats.

This ugly fish is known in some areas as the angel shark, but it is surely no angel! It is a big, brutal fish, a member of the shark family, reaching over 70lb (32kg), and has a flattened body. It spends its time on the bottom, feeding on flatfishes, other bottom-living fish, molluscs and crustaceans. The broad head has a wide mouth equipped with plenty of sharp-pointed teeth, and anglers must take care if a hooked monkfish is brought into the boat in order to remove the hook. One false move into the mouth can result in the loss of fingers.

Coloration of the monkfish is a sandy-brown on the back, with a number of blotchy markings creating a perfect camouflage to suit the ground on which the fish is lying.

A medium boat rod should be used, because of the average weight of the species, and a 30lb (13.6kg) outfit is recommended. A short wire trace is needed, about 12-18in (30-45cm), attached to a stout hook about size 8/0, the bait fished right on the bottom.

Any fish can be used for bait, with the favourites being the oily species such as mackerel and herring, but small pouting, pollack and small flatfish will do very well.

Left: *The ugly bulk of a monkfish is lifted inboard. Caught on a fish bait off the Irish coast, this specimen weighed 50lb (22.6kg).*

When mackerel is used, the best bait of all, slit the stomach to release the body fluids; these will act as an attractor. They act in the same way as rubby-dubby for shark fishing, the released matter reaching the fish's sense organs and inducing it to follow the trail to source.

Groundbaiting for monkfish is easy since the fishing is done in shallow marks. When there is a favourable tide flow the mackerel attractor should bring a monkfish or two into the range of the angler, but if necessary a real rubby-dubby method can be used to create a slick of 'interesting' matter flowing with the tide. Chopped and mashed fish in a weighted bag made of coarse, open mesh can be attached to the anchor, or lowered to the bottom with any suitable weight, even a large stone or two.

Another method is to put chopped pieces and some stones into paper bags and drop them over the side. The paper soon disintegrates and releases the fish bits. If there is a tide running, the bags should be thrown uptide.

When a monkfish takes the bait it is advisable not to hurry the strike. Play it firmly to the boat, and always be ready to give line off the spool if the fish makes a sudden plunge. When gaffing it, avoid the body of the monkfish and set the point in the wing or under the lower jaw. Here it will not cause fatal wounding and the fish can be returned alive. This is important, because the species has declined in recent years.

Below: *Despite its ray-like appearance the monkfish is in fact a shark adapted for living and feeding on the seabed.*

BREAM

Waters: Over broken ground, reefs and rocks.
Baits: Ragworm, lugworm, mussel, cockle, limpet, small fish, strips of mackerel or herring.
Techniques: Leger, paternoster, float fishing.

There are two species of bream of interest to sea anglers: the black and the red bream. Both can be caught on or close to the bottom, most bream marks being five fathoms (9m) or more deep.

Black bream
Spondyliosoma cantharus
The black bream is not really black, but has a dark grey-blue back with silvery-grey sides. The head has dark markings and the body has a strongly-marked lateral line. The brilliant colours fade soon after death, when the fish really does look black. Average weight is about 2lb (0.9kg) but specimens of 5-6lb (2.2-2.7kg) are taken regularly.

Red bream
Pagellus bogaraveo
The appearance of the red bream reflects accurately its description, being an orange-red, with a large black blotch behind the gill cover. Among the shoals there are usually fish of 5lb (2.2kg) or more, and one approaching 10lb (4.5kg) has been recorded.

Success in catching these lively fish depends largely on the size of the hook, which in turn depends on the size of the bait. The tackle should be as light as the tide and depth allow.
A simple paternoster or leger end tackle will catch plenty of fish providing the line is fine and the lead weight is just enough to keep the terminal tackle down. This allows the rig to move attractively in the current

Above right: *Paternoster tackle for bream, using two French booms which can be attached and detached without dismantling the rig.*

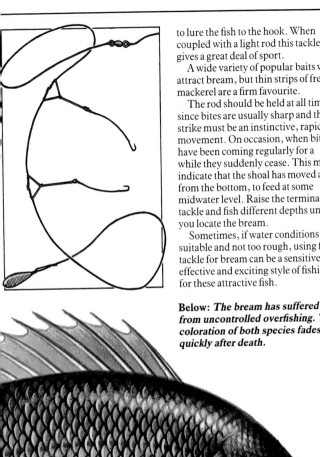

to lure the fish to the hook. When coupled with a light rod this tackle gives a great deal of sport.

A wide variety of popular baits will attract bream, but thin strips of fresh mackerel are a firm favourite.

The rod should be held at all times, since bites are usually sharp and the strike must be an instinctive, rapid movement. On occasion, when bites have been coming regularly for a while they suddenly cease. This may indicate that the shoal has moved away from the bottom, to feed at some midwater level. Raise the terminal tackle and fish different depths until you locate the bream.

Sometimes, if water conditions are suitable and not too rough, using float tackle for bream can be a sensitive, effective and exciting style of fishing for these attractive fish.

Below: *The bream has suffered from uncontrolled overfishing. The coloration of both species fades quickly after death.*

WRASSE

Waters: Inshore, rocky and weedy areas close to harbours.
Baits: Marine worms, mussel, prawn, cockle, limpet, crab, artificial lures.
Techniques: Float fishing, free-lining, paternoster, baited feathers, drift fishing.

There are seven wrasse species in northern European waters, two of which are of interest to anglers. All have longish bodies, with a single dorsal fin carrying sharp spines and a rear element of soft rays. Most are well-coloured fish, found in the vicinity of rocks. Their mouths have strong jaw teeth, capable of crushing crabs and crustaceans picked from weed-covered rocks.

Ballan wrasse
Labrus bergylta
The ballan wrasse is a fairly common fish, found close to rocky shorelines. It has an irregular pattern of brown, red and greenish-white blotches. It is the biggest of the British wrasse group, with recorded specimens of over 10lb (4.5kg).

Cuckoo wrasse
Labrus mixtus
Rarely exceeding 2lb (0.9kg), the cuckoo wrasse is a smaller species, widely distributed in offshore areas. The male is very colourful, with hues of royal blue, orange and yellow.

It is generally assumed that wrasse shoal according to their size, the shoals becoming smaller as the individual fish increase in size. When really large, wrasse become solitary, seeking food alone. The best time to fish for them seems to be on the incoming tide, when they feed.

Most wrasse fishing is done from rocks, so a long rod is more or less essential. Long casting is not necessary since the deeper water is likely to be close in, so the weight can be kept to a minimum, to match the rod. Tide will dictate the actual weight, and a beachcaster of 11ft (3.3m) will suffice. The reel should be either a multiplier or a fixed-spool loaded with a fairly strong line of about 15lb (6.8kg) b.s. to combat the wear and tear of rock fishing.

Above: *The female cuckoo wrasse (top) is surprisingly different in colour from the male (below), an unusual phenomenon among fish.*

Owing to the possibility of snagging in crevices, a length of rotten-bottom is always a wise precaution, the weaker link saving expensive tackle when it breaks.

For float fishing, a 10ft or 11ft (3-3.3m) rod, a fixed-spool reel loaded with 10-13lb (4.5-5.8kg) b.s. line and a single 2/0 hook is the standard rig. Float fishing is the better method for wrasse, for a wide area can be searched and there is little chance of the tackle snagging on the rocks.

These rocks are a danger to nylon and the line must be checked frequently for signs of abrasion.

Crab is one of the best baits, and even the hard-backed shore crab will be taken provided the shell is cracked before the bait is cast out. Half a crab is quite effective since the body contents seep away and act as an attractor. Other baits worthy of interest are lugworm, king ragworm and hermit crab.

Baited feathers are always worth trying when boat fishing and drifting slowly off a rocky coast. Another productive method is to paternoster from an anchored boat in the low-water coves, and near the thick kelp beds. Here, regular handfuls of chopped fish pieces or rubby-dubby will encourage the wrasse to feed.

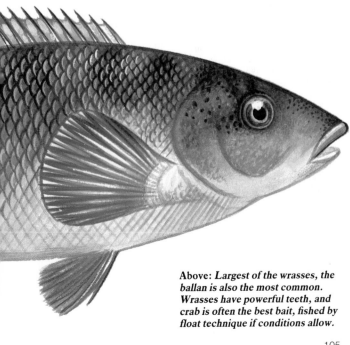

Above: *Largest of the wrasses, the ballan is also the most common. Wrasses have powerful teeth, and crab is often the best bait, fished by float technique if conditions allow.*

GURNARDS

Waters: Inshore and offshore marks, over sand and silt.
Baits: Small crabs, hermit crab, prawn, ragworm, small sandeel, thin strips of fish.
Techniques: Bottom fishing with leger tackle.

There are six species of gurnard in British waters, but only three of interest to anglers. Being all similar in habits and habitat they can be treated as one so far as tackle and tactics are concerned. All three are fairly wide in distribution and can be caught from piers and harbour walls, bays and beaches. They are also caught from boats, inshore and offshore. Usually they are hooked while the bait is being fished for other species.

Tub gurnard
Trigla lucerna
The tub is also known as the yellow gurnard, or sapphire gurnard. A southern species, it is the largest gurnard, reaching over 11lb (5kg). The deep blue of the pectoral fins is the main recognition feature. Like all gurnards it has a large head with bony plates which have sharp spines.

Grey gurnard
Eutrigla gurnardus
The commonest of these fishes, the grey gurnard is brownish-grey, with a scattering of white spots. Widely distributed, it reaches a weight of over 2lb (0.9kg).

Red gurnard
Aspitrigla cuculus
The red gurnard is not as common as

Above: *The grey gurnard, most common of these awkward-looking fish, which crawl along the seabed on their feelers searching for food.*

Below: *The tub gurnard is the largest of the six species found round the coasts of Northern Europe.*

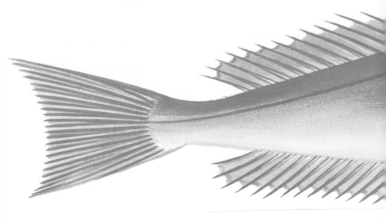

the other two. Also known as the cuckoo gurnard, this fish is more prevalent in western waters, where it is known to reach 5lb (2.2kg).

These fish crawl along the bottom using their three pairs of feelers to 'walk', searching for crustaceans to eat. They will take almost anything edible put to them. What preferences they have are confined to live prawns and live, small sandeels. Livebaits are not always available, however, so small shore crabs and hermit crabs are worth trying since they form part of the gurnards' diet. Whatever bait is used, it should be presented on a small long-shanked hook, with the barb really sharp and pointed. The tackle should always be light, governed by the tide. Leger fishing is usual.

Summer is the time when gurnards come their closest to the shore. Anglers fishing from breakwaters, piers and beaches sometimes catch them. There is no need for long casting, so use light tackle.

Drift fishing can be successful, especially a slow drift over a clean, sandy mark, the leger tackle dragging the bottom. As this disturbs the sand the gurnards are attracted to the food stirred up, and will take the bait.

When a gurnard is boated, care must be taken in handling it. The spines on the head are not poisonous, but they can inflict painful and potentially dangerous wounds.

Above: *Brightly coloured, the red gurnard is sometimes called the cuckoo gurnard. It stays inshore, but it not caught as often as the others.*

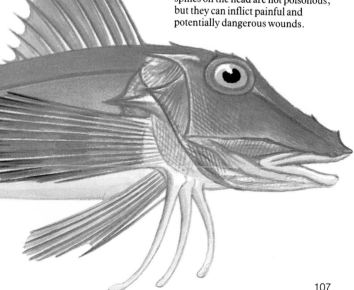

GARFISH *Belone belone*

Waters: Upper surface areas of inshore and offshore waters.
Baits: Small strips of mackerel, sprat, sandeel; small spinners.
Techniques: Free-lining, float-fishing, paternostering, spinning.

The garfish is a slim and very agile fish with a long beak-like jaw equipped with many sharp, small teeth. It is a relative of the flying fish. When live, the garfish has a coloration similar to that of the mackerel – blue-green on the back, shading to silvery on the side and belly. It is a small fish, rarely weighing more than 2lb (1kg). The summer months are the best time to seek garfish, and it is often found in the company of large mackerel shoals, both species feeding on teeming gatherings of brit and whitebait. If a garfish is hooked, it usually means that big mackerel are not far away.

Both boat anglers and shore fishermen will at times hook the garfish and if the tackle is fined down suitably great sport is to be had, the lively garfish leaping about in the spray like a miniature marlin.

Light tackle is vital if the angler is to enjoy this remarkable display. The fish will give sport out of all proportion to the size of the species, leaping clear of the water, walking on its tail, and performing 'aquabatics' at such a speed that the angler will have his time cut out keeping a tight line.

Shark anglers often catch garfish. As the rubby-dubby slick gets to work, creating a wide ribbon of oil droplets and tiny fish particles flowing downtide, it not only draws the predatory shark to the hookbait, but also attracts the hungry garfish. So the sharkmen set up a light rod, with fine line and a sliver of fresh mackerel on a

small hook. It is said that when a garfish is hooked from a sharkboat, it almost knits the shark lines.

During the garfish season, specially-designed tackle is frequently used by regular pier and breakwater anglers, particularly round the south and south-east coasts of Britain. This tackle consists of a sliding float rig, attached to the reel line by a quick-release clip after the weighted line has been cast out. The weight holds the reel line taut; the float tackle then slides down the line, allowing the bait to be fished between midwater and the surface while the line, held on the bottom, is not affected by wind or tide. This is considered to be the best method of seriously tackling garfish from piers, breakwaters, jetties and other shore projections.

Anglers fishing from a dinghy can use either rubby-dubby or chumming to attract garfish. Chum is a mixture of minced mackerel, bran, soaked bread, plus pilchard oil – a recipe similar to that used for mullet fishing. This pungent cocktail is ladled into the water at frequent intervals, and while it often puts humans off it is guaranteed to entice garfish right to the boat.

Below left: *An unmistakable fish, the gar must be fished for on light tackle. It is edible, but when cooked its bones turn green.*

Below: *The rig used by pier and breakwater anglers for garfish. A leger rig for flatfish is lowered to the seabed, and a float rig clipped on to the reel line to support the garfish bait at a higher level. Lively fish on both hooks could give the angler a few anxious moments.*

WHITING AND POUTING

Waters: Inshore and offshore, over sand and shingle (whiting); over rough ground (pouting).
Baits: Small slivers of mackerel and herring, sprat, small sandeel, mussel, squid strips, prawn, shrimp, cockle, lugworm.
Techniques: Leger, paternoster, drift-lining.

The whiting and pouting are both members of the cod family, and have the three dorsal and two anal fins which are characteristic of the cod and its relatives.

Whiting
Gadus merlangus
The whiting has an olive-green back, shading to a silvery belly. This fish has a very wide distribution, the smaller ones being found inshore while the larger ones, known as Channel whiting, are located further out in deeper water, where any fish over 4lb (1.8kg) is regarded as a fine specimen. When young, whiting feed on small inshore creatures, progressing to more substantial food, even young whiting, when adult.

Pouting
Trisopterus luscus
Also known as the bib, the pouting can be recognised by the single barbel on its chin. It is brown to dark bronze,

with vertical bands on the flanks. In southern waters it congregates in shoals and produces a bite that belies its size, leading the angler to think – and hope – that he has a much more worthwhile fish on the hook. Pouting rarely reach more than 4lb (1.8kg).

Apart from the match angler, few anglers are interesting in catching pouting, preferring more sporting species and those which provide good eating. But the matchfisherman likes to locate a shoal of pouting – or whiting – because it is likely to help him to a match-winning total. So far as tackle and tactics are concerned, the two species can be treated as one. Most of the fish are caught by boat anglers from deepwater marks.

On days when whiting and pouting are about in abundance, a two- or three-hook nylon trace fishing small baits is ideal; two or three fish can be reeled in together, one on each hook. But from boats, especially a good distance from the shore, it is the bigger whiting and pouting that are encountered and the total weight to be reeled in will be heavier.

In ideal conditions sport will continue all day, the fish feeding throughout the tide run. Usually, sport slackens when the tide flow eases, but a change of tackle from

Below: *Big whiting weigh 6lb (2.7kg) or so, but most are in the 2-3lb (1-1.3kg) range. Swimming in large shoals, they are a winter quarry.*

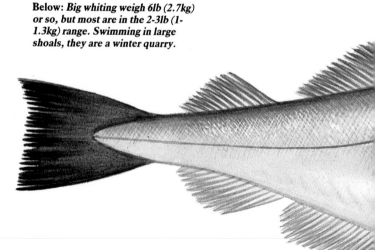

leger to paternoster, fishing small baits off the bottom, can often tempt a few hungry fish to keep the angler interested until the tide begins to flow again.

Another useful rig for these two small fishes is two hooks situated below the weight and a third up the line paternostered from a detachable French boom.

Whiting and pouting are fast biters, and their savage attacks on a bait will quickly strip the hook if it is not presented well. Large chunks of fishbait on the hook will not catch many fish, especially if the bait is old. This is because the flesh will have deteriorated and become soft, making it easy for the snapping whiting to remove it without being hooked.

To prevent this happening, use baits in good, fresh condition. Cut them into small, thin strips that sit firmly on a fine-wire 1/0 or 2/0 hook. The whole side from a single sprat, when this fish is in season, will bring the whiting and pouting to the boat if they are in the area.

When these fish are about, the bites will be fast, and it pays to hold the rod in readiness at all times. Nevertheless, it is advisable not to be too hasty in striking; the timing must be just right. Delay too long, as usually happens when the rod is propped up against the side of the boat, or on the beach rod rest, and fish will be lost.

If the located shoal is composed of mainly small whiting or pouting, it will pay to up-anchor and move in order to try to find a shoal of bigger fish. You should not need to move far, since both whiting and pouting show long-established preferences for particular areas. The experienced skipper should be aware of this and a move of perhaps no more than 100 yards or 100 metres can be enough to put the anglers in contact with a shoal of more worthwhile fish.

Above: _Whiting and pouting are often found together, but they are easily distinguished. The pouting (bottom) has a single chin barbel._

HADDOCK *Melanogrammus aeglefinus*

Waters: Offshore, over soft sand or mud. Occasionally in Scottish sea lochs where the water is very deep.
Baits: Mussel, soft crab, scallop, lugworm, mackerel, herring strip, pilchard, sprats and other small fish, artificial lures.
Techniques: Bottom fishing, paternoster, leger, pirking; while drifting or at anchor.

The haddock is credited with better fighting qualities than the larger cod, to which it is closely related. A northern species, it rarely ventures into southern waters. It is a shoal fish,

mostly taken from boats, reaching 10lb (4.5kg) and more.

The haddock has three dorsal fins and two anal fins, and a brownish back shading to a silvery belly. There is a barbel below the lower jaw. The main mark of identification is a dark spot, traditionally called a thumbprint, situated just above the pectoral fin. The tale is that the mark was made by St Peter's thumb when he lifted the fish from the sea.

Although found in the North Sea, the cold waters round the Scottish coast provide the best opportunities for catching haddock. Boat fishing is

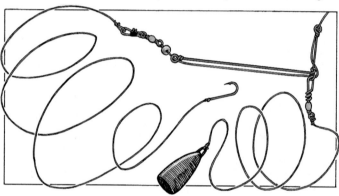

Above: *A deepwater paternoster rig for haddock. Deep water requires heavy weights, and the length of the hook trace depends on the tide.*

Below: *Shoaling in huge numbers, the haddock is found in the deep, cold northern waters off the coasts of Scotland and Iceland.*

probably the only way to find them, at least half a mile from the shore.

A rod of about 10ft (3m), in the 20lb (9kg) class, with a reel such as a Penn 4/0 is ideal. The reel may seem to be excessively large, but it is necessary because of the depth of water, and the thickness of the line. This will be of 20lb b.s., a strength dictated by the weight of lead needed to get the bait down to the seabed.

End tackle is a basic single-hook paternoster, with a trace varying from 3ft (1m) in slack water to 8ft (2.4m) when a strong tide is running. Hooks can be 2/0 or 3/0, baited with any of the items listed above, bearing in mind that haddock prefer a soft bait. This is why mussel and lugworm prove effective. The baits can be used singly or as a cocktail – two different baits on the same hook.

The single-hook trace is fitted to the reel line above the weight, and if required another hook link can be added further up. Unless you are fishing a definite, known mark, these rigs can be fished from a drifting boat, with the baits kept as close to the bottom as possible. Snagging, of course, is always possible, so a 'rotten bottom' weight should be used.

Haddock have a habit of playing about or nibbling at the bait for quite a while before mouthing it. Therefore it is wise not to strike at the first tremble of the rod tip. When the haddock finally takes, the rod top will be pulled down hard; this is the time to strike.

The haddock is a fish with a soft mouth, which means that hooks can sometimess pull free, so always use a net to get it inboard.

Above left: *Irish waters also hold haddock. This specimen-sized fish was caught from a drifting boat out of Kilalla Bay on a charter trip.*

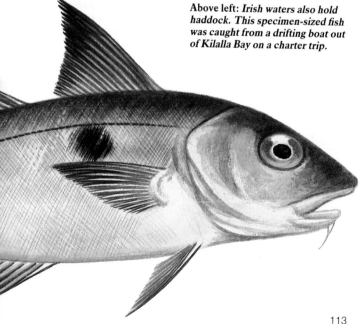

HAKE *Merluccius merluccius*

Waters: Mainly deep offshore marks.
Baits: Live mackerel, herring, sandeel, and fillets of these and other fish.
Techniques: Running leger, paternoster leger, free-lining, drift fishing, pirking.

Although a member of the cod family, the hake is a rather slender fish. There are two dorsal fins, one at the rear running for more than half the length of the fish to the tail, the anal fin equalling it in length. The fish has a large head, and numerous teeth. The eyes are large, Colour is a slate grey on the back, shading to a silvery underside. This a deepwater fish, growing to about 4ft (1.2m) long and weighing over 30lb (13.6kg), but any fish over 10lb (4.5kg) is a good size.

Boat fishing is essential, because hake rarely venture inshore. They are regarded as a deepwater species, but they can swim at different levels, moving up from the bottom to feed on sprats, and other small fish. Because they are predators, live or dead fish make the best baits.

A rod of the 20-30lb (9-13.6kg) class will be suitable, mounted with a large multiplier big enough to hold the amount of line needed to fish deepwater marks.

A paternoster terminal tackle is the best rig, carrying one or two hooks. The main trace is the lower one, long

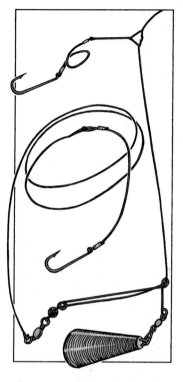

Above: *A paternoster rig for hake, with two wire traces. The upper trace is attached to a French boom, while the lower is linked to the reel line. The weight is clipped to a 6in (15cm) wire boom.*

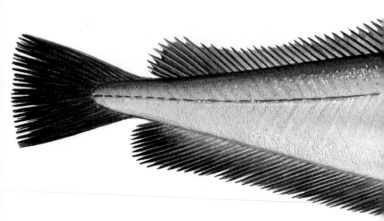

Above: *A fine 11½lb (5.2kg) hake taken by a boat angler off the south coast of Cornwall. Note the large, well-equipped jaws.*

and flowing, with a 4/0 or 6/0 hook attached to the end of the reel line by a wire trace or hook link about 6-12in (15-30cm) long. The weight depends on the strength of tide at the time.

Bait the main hook with a live fish, and the second hook with a small dead fish or a large fillet of mackerel. Hook the livebait near the tail, so it moves naturally and attractively.

Fishing may be done at anchor, but when the sea is too deep drift fishing is the only alternative. An advantage of this is that a large area can be covered if the fish are not immediately apparent. Drifting also allows the use of the pirk, baited or unbaited. This lure often works when fish baits are ignored. Night fishing for hake is often very rewarding.

Below: *Essentially a deepwater fish, the hake rarely ventures inshore. It has become relatively uncommon following overfishing by trawlers.*

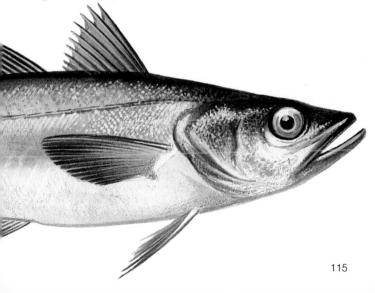

INDEX

USEFUL ADDRESSES

Bass Anglers Sport Fishing Society, Mrs Diana Rowles, 58 Sycamore Avenue, Hillingbury, Chandlers Ford, Hants

British & European Line-Class Angling Club, Ray Rush, Secretary, 10 Southcote Road, Tufnell Park, London N19 5BJ

British Record (rod-caught) Fish Committee, 11 Cowgate, Peterborough PE1 1LZ
Tel: 0733 54084

Estuarine and Brackish Water Sciences Association, c/o R. S. K. Barnes, Department of Zoology, University of Cambridge, Downing Street, Cambridge CB2 3EJ

European Federation of Sea Anglers (English section), R. J. Norman, Moorlands, Bagshot Road, Knaphill, Woking, Surrey

Halibut Club of Great Britain, Secretary, c/o Caithness Tourist Association, 1 Francis Street, Wick, Caithness

Irish Federation of Sea Anglers, Hugh O'Rourke, Secretary, 67 Windsor Drive, Monsktown, Co. Cublin, Ireland

Marine Conservation Society, Candle Cottage, Kempley, Dymock, Gloucestershire

National Anglers Council, Peter Tombleson OBE, 11 Cowgate, Peterborough
PE1 1LZ   Tel: 0733 54084

National Federation of Sea Anglers, Bob Page, Secretary, 26 Downview Crescent, Uckfield, Sussex TN22 1UB   Tel: 0825 3589

Scottish Federation of Sea Anglers, Mrs C. Watson, Secretary, 18 Ainslie Place, Edinburgh EH3 6AU

Scottish Marine Biological Association, Dunstaffnage Marine Research Laboratory, PO Box 3, Oban, Argyll PA34 4AD

Sea Anglers Match Federation, Alan Yates, Secretary, 1 Great Pineham Farm Cottages, Pineham, Kent CT15 5HA   Tel: 0304 820162

Sea Angling Liaison Committee of Great Britain & Ireland, 11 Cowgate, Peterborough PE1 1LZ

Shark Angling Club of Great Britain, Secretary, The Quay, East Looe, Cornwall
PL13 1DX   Tel: 05036 2642

The British Conger Club, R. H. J. Quest, Secretary, 5 Hill Crest, Mannamead, Plymouth

Underwater Association, c/o J. Shand, Department of Zoology, University of Bristol, Woodland Road, Bristol BS8 1UG

Welsh Federation of Sea Anglers, G. Howen, Secretary, 11 Stafford Road, Newport, Gwent

PICTURE CREDITS

Copyright of the artwork illustrations on the pages following the artists' names is the property of Salamander Books Ltd.

Keith Linsell: 15, 32, 34, 35, 37, 39, 40, 42, 43, 44, 46, 50, 54, 62, 80, 82, 90, 93 (top and bottom), 98 (top and bottom), 103 (top), 109, 112 (top), 114 (top).
Colin Newman (Linden Artists): 20-21
Eric Tenney: 52-53, 56-57, 60-61, 64-65, 66-67, 70-71, 74-75, 78-79, 81, 85, 88-89, 92, 96-97, 100-101, 102-103, 104-105, 106-107, 108-109, 110-111, 112-113, 114-115

Photographs
All the photographs in this book are by Bill Howes except the following:
Trevor Housby: 63, 95
Mike Millman: Front cover, 75, 115
© Salamander Books Ltd: 19 (bottom), 51
Shakespeare Company: 11 (bottom left, bottom right)